Honda
GOLD WING

Honda

An American Japanese motorcycle

Peter Rae

OSPREY

First published mid 1984 by Osprey Publishing Limited
12–14 Long Acre, London WC2E 9LP
Member company of the George Philip Group
First reprint summer 1984
Second reprint spring 1985

Sole distributors for the USA

Motorbooks International
Publishers & Wholesalers Inc
Osceola, Wisconsin 54020, USA

British Library Cataloguing in Publication Data

Rae, Peter
  Honda Gold Wing.
  I. Honda Gold Wing motorcycle—History
  I. Title
  629.2.275   TL448.H6

ISBN 0-85045-567-7

Editor Tim Parker
Design Norman Brownsword
Filmset by Tameside Filmsetting Ltd
Ashton-under-Lyne, Lancs
Printed in Hong Kong

Contents

Acknowledgements

The author wishes to thank the following for their kind assistance in producing this book: Roly Batchelor, *Bike* magazine, Mike Bridge, Chris Bryant, Bob Doornbos of American Honda, Roger Etcell of Honda UK, Paul Hildebrand, Roger Hull, Ken Hull, Martin Langford, Adrian Mackay, Malcolm Newell, Toshio Nozue, Bruce Preston, Kevin Radley, Shuji Tanaka and Larry Tietz.

To Wing Nuts everywhere.

Introduction

When breakfast is just a memory 300 miles behind your tail light and supper still a dream 300 miles beyond the horizon, life's complexities boil down to a few simple but crucial issues: how fresh is your mind, how sore is your backside, how stiff is your body, how well is your bike running and how much fuel is in the tank. Weighty issues such as who makes the fastest-accelerating superbike, who will win the next election, Soviet foreign policy and the political future of the Middle East all assume a wonderful irrelevance.

At times like these, the make and model of motorcycle you're pointing in the general direction of dinner becomes of more than passing interest. There was a time when riding 600 miles or more in a day was the preserve of an optimistic, masochistic minority of courageous Harley owners and a wealthy minority who could afford a BMW. Touring over even more modest distances still meant having to endure varying degrees of discomfort through vibration or noise, the

The 1975 GL1000 delighted some, horrified others. Ten years and more than 300,000 sales later, the Gold Wing has a cult following and is still the yardstick by which all touring motorcycles are judged

inevitability of daily rear chain adjustment on the bigger bikes, and the likelihood of mechanical trauma on many smaller ones. Even the glamorous and expensive flat twins from Bavaria assaulted the rider's ears with tappet noise, despite being otherwise well equipped for continent-hopping.

Honda went a long way toward solving the problem in 1969 with the scene-stealing CB750. It was relatively smooth, plenty powerful, reliable, quiet and sophisticated, and touring riders took to the world's highways on the new four in huge numbers. But the CB750 was a mite too tall for many riders, it suffered a little from tingly vibration and it possessed an enormous appetite for final drive chains.

A lot of riders wished for a CB750 with shaft drive to overcome the problem. But by 1972 a far grander solution was taking shape, a motorcycle which would have as great an impact on the future of motorcycle touring as the CB750 itself had on the whole future of motorcycle design.

The Honda Gold Wing was first shown to a largely incredulous public at the Cologne Motorcycle Show in Germany in October 1974. For months in advance, the motorcycle press had been spreading rumours of a new shaft-driven Honda, a watercooled Honda, a 1000 cc Honda, a flat-four Honda. Yet few people seemed prepared for what finally appeared in Cologne: a motorcycle of gargantuan proportions combining in a single machine not only all the rumoured features but a whole lot more besides.

The paper specification alone went some way towards justifying the characteristic mid-70's optimism of Honda's publicity chiefs as they built a lavish promotional campaign around their new creation. They were bold enough to dub it the ultimate motorcycle. But if they expected the world's

In America, touring riders looked on the new Honda as a basis on which to build a bolt-on dream. The Windjammer fairing and custom seat on this K3 were typical additions

motorcycle press corps and the massed armies of motorcycle enthusiasts to fete them universally for their stunning achievement, they were in for a surprise.

Initial reaction was mixed, with the American press generally giving the Wing more favourable reviews than the European. In probably the first-ever test, published in April 1975, the authoritative American journal *Cycle* praised the Wing concept, lauded its straight-line performance, admired its engine technology and was not uncomplimentary about its handling. 'We don't know exactly how much the GL1000 is going to cost,' *Cycle* said, 'but however much it turns out to be, it'll be a bargain in terms of utter engine smoothness and quietness, in terms of the quality of engineering and new-wave thinking that has gone into it, in terms of surprisingly agile handling performance, and shattering stopping and accelerating performance. Here is a tourer, unblurred and brilliantly focused for those who want nothing to intrude on their feeling of the road and who want to intrude on no one else as they enjoy it.'

Honda's designers and publicity folk could have wished for no greater accolade from the world's most respected monthly motorcycle magazine. In Europe, too, the Wing was well received by some writers but ridiculed by others. *Motor Cycle Weekly* said: 'If ever there was a definitive touring machine combining effortless power with stately manners—this is it. In spite of its weight, it steers and handles as well as many 750s.' The respected and generally conservative *Motorcycle Sport* said: 'It offers almost every refinement that the discerning motorcyclist could wish for, is comfortable, extremely rapid, acceptably economical and, above all, exciting to ride. It also rates as the quietest and smoothest motorcycle we have tried. We nominate the GL1000 as the big touring bike of 1975.' (The man who wrote that was a card-carrying BMW owner.)

But the very attributes of smoothness, quietness and sophistication that made the Wing stand out from the crowd were its undoing in the eyes of some European testers who still clung to the belief that *real* motorcycles should be a little wild. The most damning condemnation of the GL1000 came in a 1976 road-test in *Bike*, the irreverent British monthly which was increasingly influential among younger riders. The headline on the *Bike* test asked simply: 'Two-wheeled motor car?'

That, in a sense, is what Honda had produced. Until 1975, few motorcycles could attempt to match a car's ability to transport even two people and their luggage across a continent in relative comfort and cleanliness and with no more attention than regular visits to the fuel pump. The introduction of the Gold Wing changed all that. Those riders who saw the 'two-wheeled car' tag as a term of derision simply bought a different motorcycle. But more than 300,000 riders (260,000 of them in the United States) saw the description as a compliment and bought the Gold Wing. They made the Gold Wing the single motorcycle model with probably the most loyal following of all time. This book is their story and the story of the motorcycle they ride.

1 The King of Motorcycles

Forerunner of the Gold Wing and the CBX1000: the 1973 Honda AOK flat six never went into production. Note the BMW seat, mufflers, shock absorbers, drive shaft, rear hub and gearbox

In the autumn of 1972 a small group of engineers and designers filed into one of the many little committee rooms in Honda's factory at Wako in southern Japan. A Western observer would have noticed nothing remarkable about the room; it was clean and modern like a dozen others in the sprawling motorcycle research and development centre, with a long meeting table and a spotless blackboard built into an end wall.

Around that table were the men, some of them still in their twenties, who had brought the world such diverse motorcycles as the CB125 twin and the mighty CB750 four. The man at the head of the table was Soichiro Irimajiri, the brilliant Honda engineer who in later years was to give us the hugely successful CX500 vee-twin and the thrilling CBX1000 six.

But on this morning in 1972, Mr Irimajiri had other things on his mind. Since the innovative Honda 750 four had swept all before it following its launch in 1969, other powerful machines had overtaken it in outright performance and sheer prestige. Among them were the all-conquering

Kawasaki Z1 and the BMW R90S. The CB750, sophisticated and desirable though it was, could no longer uphold Honda's corporate pride against such formidable opposition. What was needed, Irimajiri told his colleagues, was a new Honda which would be recognized and acclaimed as the King of Motorcycles, the world's fastest and best grand tourer.

The motorcycle which this little band of designers came up with was like no bike ever seen before. The Honda AOK, the prototype world-beater, was a flat-six, single-overhead-cam 1470 cc monster. It weighed in at a comparatively light 484 lb (220 Kg), had a bore of 72 mm and a stroke of 60 mm, ran a compression ratio of 8.0 to 1, breathed through a downdraught two-barrel carburettor and developed a modest-enough 80 bhp at 6700 rpm. It had a wheelbase of 1480 mm, carried a 20-litre fuel tank, wore a 4.00 × 18 rear tyre and 3.25 × 19 front, turned in 12-second standing-start quarter-miles and topped out at 130 mph (220 km/h).

The AOK borrowed heavily from existing designs. It had a cradle frame with engine mountings like those of the CB750. It featured shaft final drive and, not surprisingly, the rear end bore a striking resemblance to a BMW. Only one prototype was built, and test riders reported that the engine was 'dead smooth' throughout the rev range. They said it had 'lots of power' and felt extremely stable thanks to its low centre of gravity. The main drawback was the sheer length of the flat-six power unit which made a decent riding position impossible to achieve, so the AOK was consigned to the list of motorcycles the world never saw.

The corporate will to build the King of Motorcycles continued to prevail however, but Honda felt that a more practical approach lay in a flat-four engine

The AOK was abandoned in favour of the shorter flat four layout which has lasted through ten years of continual refinement and development. Honda designers had created 'a motorcycle for the thinking motorcyclist'

layout. The engineer who took over from Irimajiri as project leader for the new flat-four was Toshio Nozue, a frame designer who had been responsible for the CB750 project from the outset and had the two-stroke 250 cc off-road Honda Elsinore to his credit.

Nozue and his team developed their concept of a world-beating grand tourer into a prototype flat-four with water cooling, belt-driven single overhead camshafts, four carburettors, a displacement of 999 cc, a power output of 80 bhp at 7500 rpm, five-speed gearbox and a whole bunch of clever ideas brought together for the first time in one motorcycle.

Honda thought of their new creation as the first watercooled bike, but of course the British-built Scott had been down that route decades before. Nor was it the first machine to carry its fuel supply underneath the seat. But it was the first to use the AC generator as a contra-rotating flywheel to counteract the inherent torque reaction of the in-line crankshaft.

As far as Mr Nozue is concerned, overcoming that torque reaction was the only real engineering challenge in developing the new Honda. Any other minor difficulties were no more than the experienced design team would expect in developing any new engine.

'The initial reaction of our test riders was that the low centre of gravity gave the motorcycle excellent stability and resistance to side winds,' says Nozue today. 'In other words, it was a very good touring machine. The engine was very quiet, even with a fairing fitted, and it was very powerful. However, it did have a certain lack of torque at low speeds. And the testers reported that kickstarting was difficult, that their feet came in contact with the engine and got hot too easily, and that the machine was very difficult to pick up if it fell over.'

From final prototype to production model, virtually nothing was changed. But most buyers disliked the hard, flat seat, the rear suspension, and the rust-prone exhaust system. Later, all would be changed

That apart, the prototype went down well with the development riders. To get the finished product absolutely right, and fit for its role as the new King, the machine went through a year of testing at Honda's Tochigi test facility, compared with the more usual eight months. When it finally hit the showrooms in 1975 as the Honda Gold Wing GL1000 KO, only three items had been redesigned from the prototype: the self-cancelling turn signals had been abolished, the radiator cap had been altered for safety reasons, and a warning sticker was added to its top. That was the sum total of the changes; the designers, it seemed, had got it right first time.

Subsequent redesign in successive model years was to show that even the King of Motorcycles could stand improving here and there, but essentially the design team had achieved its prime objective from the outset.

'We felt we had succeeded in creating in the GL series a motorcycle that appealed to the thinking motorcyclist,' says Nozue. 'We saw the Harley-Davidson as being for the hippies and the Hell's Angels. And the BMW was a sporty bike best suited to short-distance touring. The GL was a true long-distance tourer.'

He laughs at the suggestion, rife in the press in 1975, that Honda spent £500,000 (over $1 million at 1975 exchange rates) developing the rear tyre for the Gold Wing. 'No, we didn't spend half a million pounds,' he grins. 'But Honda does have the tyre manufacturers develop a special tyre for every motorcycle model we produce. And the problems of developing a rear tyre for the Gold Wing were, it goes without saying, somewhat greater than for other bikes.'

One area where Honda was hopelessly optimistic was in its sales forecasts for the GL series. In 1975, the year of the launch, they sold 5000 Wings against a target of 60,000. The problem was more one of poor target-setting than public disenchantment with the new superbike. The new arrival was greeted with enthusiasm in some sections of the world's motorcycle press, but praise was not unanimous.

2 A two-wheeled car?

The research done, the plans drawn, the prototypes made and tested and modified, production underway, Honda launched the Gold Wing into a largely unsuspecting world marketplace. It was a market which had altered dramatically over a short period of time, a volatile market which had seen a succession of new motorcycles introduced in rapid order, each one bigger, faster, zappier and more mind-blowing than the last.

Ever since the launch of the CB750 in 1969, or possibly the launch of the Kawasaki 500 triple the year before, technological wizardry had been coming at the performance-orientated motorcyclist thick and fast: the Kawasaki 750 triple, the ill-fated Yamaha TX750 twin, the Laverda 1000 triple, the desmo Ducati vee-twin, the Moto Guzzi vee-twin, the Norton Interstate (no relation!), the electric-start Triumph T160 Trident, the MV Agusta 750 four, the Suzuki 750 triple, the BMW R90S, and, perhaps most significantly, the Kawasaki Z1. To a world which still thought the CB750 was pretty neat and pretty desirable, the concept of 80-bhp one-litre bikes was exciting, to say the

least. Each new model was as much a corporate statement of the factory's capabilities as it was a practical motorcycle in its own right. And don't forget that by 1975 a lot of riders were saying: 'Imagine a bike with the Z1's power that didn't eat chains for lunch and actually handled but didn't cost as much as a European superbike.'

Against that background, Honda introduced the new GL1000 KO Gold Wing. It was launched separately in each major world market. This was before the days when Honda and all the other major manufacturers would fly the world's motorcycle press editors to some exotic location to push out the boat for some new machine. In Britain, the motorcycle press first got to ride the Wing at TT time in 1975. Honda (UK) Ltd brought a handful of the new monsters to the Isle of Man and let selected journalists ride them for a few miles. Reaction was mixed. Some diehards dismissed the beast as a gross miscarriage of motorcycle design. The Wing, they said, was too heavy, too complicated, too big, unnecessary, and too much like a two-wheeled car—Lead not Gold, even. Others were impressed by the ease with which such a heavy machine could be ridden but nevertheless agreed that it was too heavy to be taken seriously. Still others saw it in more or less the same terms as Honda did: an exciting, trend-setting motorcycle with more power than any predecessor, more sophistication, more features, more everything—all for considerably less

Many Gold Wing design studies resulted in a more rounded, bulbous appearance which had more in common with road-going Jawas and CZs than with anything from Honda. Compare this with the lighter-looking production model

than a BMW R90S.

Everybody who rode the Wing, however, commented favourably on its uncanny smoothness, its formidable straight-line acceleration and its appetite for eating up the miles. But attitudes immediately polarized in pro-Wing and anti-Wing camps. Perhaps the two viewpoints are best illustrated by two British road-tests of the period. One is reprinted by kind permission of *Bike*, the other is from the now defunct *Motorcyclist Illustrated*. The former magazine was probably the most controversial and the most avidly read motorcycle magazine in Britain in the mid-1970s. To *Bike*, nothing was sacred. Launched in the early 1970s, it had brought a breath of fresh air to the UK press scene and by 1975 it was in its heyday. *Motorcyclist Illustrated*, on the other hand, was basically an upmarket magazine which tried to capture the flavour of its subject from the viewpoint of experienced and enthusiastic freelance journalists. It was at that time the most touring-orientated motorcycle magazine in Britain. Here are the unabridged road tests, starting with *Bike*.

Two-Wheeled Motor Car? The muted, muffled, de-toxed, idiot-proofed motorcycle is with us in the shape of Honda's Gold Wing. Bill Haylock remains unimpressed.

This prototype is much nearer the final version. Honda designed the GL as a 999 cc bike from the start, so the GX750 tag was merely to fool curious onlookers and snoopers

When is a motorcycle not a motorcycle? No, that's not a cue for any facetious answers—I'm getting seriously worried at the direction the development of Japanese bikes is taking.

OK, we owe Mr Honda a lot for past services. He and his competitors have done wonders for small cube bikes and made us realise that big roadburners don't *have* to shake or leak oil. But I have an uneasy feeling that, as far as big bikes are concerned, the Japs are starting to go over the top. They're trying to turn bikers into socially acceptable two wheeled motorists.

When Honda's Gold Wing became more than just a well engineered rumour, Honda's publicity machine rumbled into action like a squadron of Chieftain tanks, hoping to conquer the prestige bike market with battle cries like:

'Quite simply the most advanced motorcycle ever made.

'Acclaimed as the most significant and major achievement in the motorcycle industry for many years . . .

'The Ultimate . . .'

Powerful stuff, even to the experienced connoisseurs of public relations bullshit. Just about everyone did what was required, and obediently gasped in wonder, instead of asking the question, 'The Ultimate what?'

No one looked too closely at the brash claims, which in actual fact, don't stand too much scrutiny. The flat four motor is nothing new to motorcycles, nor is water cooling, nor is shaft drive, nor is the dummy tank, nor is the rear disc brake. One of the biggest, fastest, most complex and impressive motor cycles ever made the Gold Wing may be, but the most advanced . . . ?

In truth, the Gold Wing is a very conventional motorcycle. It is remarkable not so much for technological innovation, as for the change of course it represents, away from traditional motorcycle technology and into line with contemporary automobile technology. It also reflects Honda's avowed policy of making the motorcycle more socially acceptable and safer, even if it also makes them more boring.

Another design exercise shows the rolling chassis almost finalised, but the stylists were still experimenting with different tank, seat and sidepanel shapes

OK, so it can't be a bad thing if bikes get cleaner, quieter and safer (although I've got doubts whether they are getting safer). But I object to a manufacturer deciding that he'll design what he thinks I ought to have rather than what I want. Yeah, of course he'll point out that I don't have to buy a Honda or whatever, but the trouble is, a company as big as Honda can influence the direction the whole of the bike world takes, and the dissenters end up having no choice.

You can't blame the manufacturers too much though, Honda are only conscientiously trying to anticipate future legislation. The Gold Wing's under-seat petrol tank, for example, may become a legal obligation on all new bikes before long, if proposals for new Common Market regulations are accepted. The Wing is muted, muffled, de-toxed, idiot-proofed and generally made fit for human consumption, according to the protectors of the public well-being throughout the world.

Right, so having explained that Honda's design judgement is partly influenced by politicians, what are they aiming at anyway? Their current Stateside adverts bill the Gold Wing as: 'The epitome of what touring is all about'. Well, certainly you couldn't pretend the Gold Wing is a sports machine. Although it is one of the fastest production motorcycles in a straight line its handling characteristics and weight are enough to dissuade any hard 'sporting' riders.

But when you start examining the Gold Wing's attributes as a tourer, it falls short on one or two important counts. After riding it for the first couple of days I was at a loss to know exactly what role the Wing actually fulfills. Then a realisation slowly crystallised after a few more days riding around, the Honda drawing crowds wherever it was parked. It's an image bike, pure and simple. It ain't meant to be functional—it's just meant to swell your head. It's for the guy who loves spending half an hour every time he stops to fill up, explaining to the impressionable onlookers about how his bike's got four water-cooled cylinders, with belt driven camshafts, and shaft drive . . . an' if you peer in there behind the radiator you can see the cooling fan—just like a car. Car

The modellers experimented with many different tank styles. This one may look awful, but if it held petrol it would have given the Wing a welcome boost in touring range

drivers love the Gold Wing, they'll stand and stare at it for ages. It's something they can relate to.

Personally I find the gas station inquisitions a little tedious when I just want to get out and ride. And I'm rambling on and on and you just want to know what it is like when you get out there and ride it, right?

Well, first impressions are striking, I mean, it's so huge that whether you like the way it looks or not, you can't help but be intrigued. First time I saw one in the flesh, it was parked beside a Suzuki 750 triple. Now, the GT750 always struck me as a hunky motorcycle, built along the same lines as a Russian ladies' champion shotputter. But the Gold Wing made the Suzy look positively dainty. Yep, H-D's big mutha of them all, the Electra Glide, has a rival at last.

But once you clamber aboard, the Gold Wing seems to shrink to more manageable proportions, and the overall impression is favourable, because it's not the beast you were expecting. It rolls on and off the centre stand effortlessly, compared to some big bikes I've experienced, and off the stand the weight feels far less intimidating than I'd expected. Keeping the centre of gravity down low helps disguise the 650 lbs tanked-up weight remarkably well.

Next nice surprise is the smoothness of the motor. I was expecting a flat four to feel smooth, but it's a revelation as soon as you punch the starter button and the motor hums quietly away as you warm it up at a fast idle. And when I blipped the throttle

In the modelling shop, a sidepanel receives some final adjustments. A cobra's-head fuel tank was obviously intended as a fuel carrier; the concept of a dummy tank came later

there was no trace of that lurching torque reaction, known so well to BMW and Guzzi owners, because the Honda's contra-rotating alternator compensates for it.

The Gold Wing is so amazingly quiet too. Huge, ugly silencers mute the exhaust note to a gentle off-beat burble, and the water jacket surrounding the cylinders effectively muffles all mechanical noise, apart from a peculiar whistle from the camshafts' toothed rubber drive belts.

High, wide bars help you manhandle the brute through traffic with deceptive ease and I felt confident right away, even in rush hour London traffic. Trickling along at walking pace is no problem as the bike is so well balanced, and although there's a slight hint of the snatchiness characteristic of all Honda motors fitted with CV carbs, the heavy flywheel minimises its effect.

Power delivery is smooth and tractable, although not as torquey as you'd expect from a big incher. In fact, like all Hondas maximum torque is high up the rev range at six and a half grand, and you have to use all those revs and more to really get a move on. But the Gold Wing has the cubes and the flywheel weight to make slow riding leisurely.

The drive isn't as direct as on Bee Ems and Guzzis, probably because the Honda's drive train is not direct through from the crankshaft. It has chain primary drive (of Morse, not roller variety) from the crankshaft down to the gearbox which lies underneath the crankshaft. That makes gear-changing altogether more pleasant than on most shaft driven bikes, except for the fact that it had a disturbing tendency to miss changes at high revs.

This early drawing of the GL engine is more rounded than the real thing. It also bears the legend 'GL750' to keep everyone guessing. No wonder we heard so many rumours of a water-cooled 750 from Honda

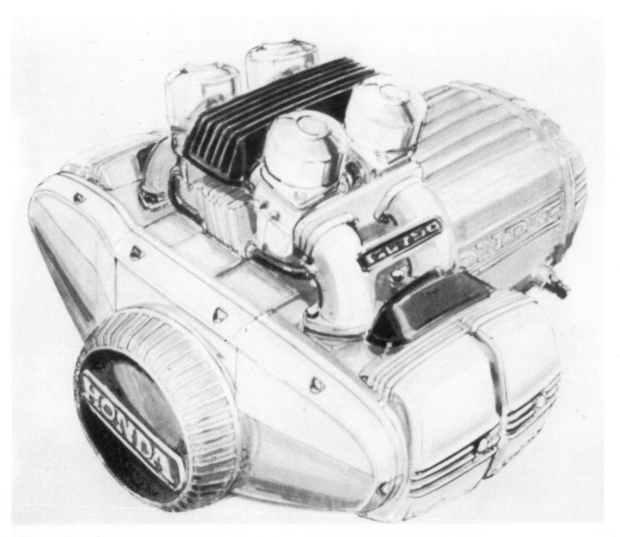

Nothing really unpleasant rears its head until you start trying to go round corners. The steering is pretty heavy of course, but it does have some rather more disturbing quirks both at low and high speeds. More about that later.

My first chance to let it all out was up the M1, the sort of environment where the Gold Wing is at its best, in fact, the only place where it really makes any sense. I began to think maybe it should be billed as the world's most luxurious drag racer; its performance in a straight line is phenomenal.

The Gold Wing is one of the fastest bikes we've tested, on top speed and acceleration, despite the enormous handicap of the flabby excess weight it has to lug around. The motor, so Honda say, kicks out 80 horses. Well, it's enough to catapult you towards the horizon with thoroughly indecent haste accompanied by the shriek and smell of incinerated rubber.

But what is most amazing about the Wing's performance is the effortlessness of it all. Lack of vibration had a lot to do with it. The only time the motor transmits a buzz is on the overrun as you shut off. While it's pulling the power comes on out smoothly right up to the 8,500 rpm red zone on the tacho. There's nothing fierce about the power. It just surges forward like an avalanche when you twist open the taps, and then suddenly things get noticeably more hectic as the needle approaches the 7,000 rpm power peak.

The bike is perfectly capable, I'm sure, of cruising at a steady 110, only trouble is the rider isn't. High speed straight line stability is excellent and at that speed revs are nowhere near the red, but the riding position prohibits you from making the most of the Wing's over-the-ton cruising capabilities. Ten minutes at that sort of speed and you begin to feel the subject of some infernal medieval torture as the wind tries to wrench your arms from their sockets. Fitting narrower, flat bars would make speed more practical, but then the Wing would be a pig in town. Only way to win is to fit a fairing.

I feel that if you can't use all the performance a powerful and expensive bike provides, then it's all a bit of a waste. But the Gold Wing is so smooth and comfortable

The cobra's-head design makes it on to a prototype—but not for long. The seat and 750-style four-into-four chrome exhaust arrangement looks neat, though. Note the pod for a tank-top fuel gauge

down nearer the legal limit on the motorway that I really enjoyed the first part of the test cruising along the M1 and A1. Apart from the frustration of frequent fuel stops, that is.

To limit the range of a luxury touring bike by providing a fuel capacity which is quite inadequate for long distance travelling seems foolish to me. And the Honda's four gallons is inadequate, related to its heavy fuel consumption—a bit over 30 mpg, and even lower if you really use the motor's urge. The fuel gauge is really worse than useless—it just frightens you by reminding you how rapidly the juice is burning. Anyway, if you stop to fill up when the needle gets to the red you only get 80 miles between service stations, but after a while I learned to ignore it and follow the normal practice of tanking up as soon as possible after switching on to reserve. That way the interval between fill-ups was extended to 100 or 110 miles during fast motorway cruising—still nowhere near enough. A realistic range would be more like 200 miles. It ought to be possible to stash away that much petrol on the Gold Wing, even under the saddle, if Honda had laid things out more sensibly.

The dummy tank is poorly thought out and wastes a tremendous amount of space. OK, it impresses people when the thing unfolds to display assorted electrical gubbins, the air cleaner, radiator header tank and starting lever, but to me it's a joke that displays the worst of Japanese gizmo-mania. If they'd designed it seriously Honda could have squeezed it all into half the space, and left room for the battery and the rest of the electronics so the space they presently occupy behind the side panels could have been filled with fuel.

So much for its failings as a motorway cruiser. When you start using the Wing on any other kind of road, rather more fundamental and frightening failings begin to show. The Gold Wing is the only bike that has caused me to analyse its handling characteristics in terms usually associated with those nauseating, key-jangling four-wheeled pseuds normally found discussing Mini Coopers and Cortina GTs in the

Now dubbed the GX1000, this prototype features a single, heavily drilled front disc brake—this was 1974, long before Honda started offering drilled or slotted discs—tiny side-panels, yet another seat and a tank style that was to be adopted later for smaller machines

lounge bars of Watney pubs.

But the Honda's massive bulk produces peculiar handling traits I've not come across on other bikes. On fast bends it has a distinct tendency to understeer—the inertia of all that weight tries to make the bike continue in a straight line, with the result that the bike takes the bends on a much wider line than you'd intended. Bumps add an extra twist, quite literally, by producing a sort of wallowing motion at the back end. On top of that, the centre stand grounds far too easily.

At slow speeds, the cornering characteristics are reversed and the bike oversteers, needing a fair pressure against the end of the bars to the inside of the bend, to keep to the desired course. It feels as though the weight is trying to make the bike flop over on its side.

Part of the problem seems to be the way Honda's designers indiscriminately bend tubes around various awkward bits that happen to get in the way, like the radiator. Most Japanese manufacturers have always seemed to have a rather empirical approach to frame building, but the way the front down tubes splay out just below the steering head to wrap around the radiator, seems to defy both science and common sense.

Part of the problem too, is in the suspension. The springing seems too hard, while the damping is too soft, producing a ride that is both harsh and poorly controlled over bumps. Maybe I was over critical because the last bike I'd ridden was the BMW R90S, which has things supremely well sorted in that department. But then the Gold Wing is competing in exactly the same field . . .

But the greatest problem of all with the Wing's handling is the massive weight, which is far more than a conventional motorcycle chassis and suspension should have to cope with. I think there is no excuse for a bike to weigh much over 500 lbs, even a sophisticated luxury tourer, and ideally it should weigh less. BMW's R90S is almost 200 lbs lighter than the Gold Wing, and is a much better motorcycle because of it.

All that extra weight and complexity makes you wonder whether the advantages

Now we see twin discs up front, chrome radiator trims, a move to black exhausts, and a tank style reminiscent of the CB350 Four. The model designation has changed to GL1000

aren't outweighed by the penalties incurred because of the extra weight. That superfluous hundredweight and a half drags down the performance to the level of a good, light 750, negating the Wing's 250 cc advantage, and yet you pay the penalty of higher fuel consumption, poor handling and rapid tyre wear. That last point is one well worth considering. The rear tyre of the test bike was worn down to the legal minimum of 1 mm tread depth after a recorded mileage of 2,400 miles. Half a dozen wheelspinning standing quarter runs hadn't helped, but on the other hand that mileage included the running-in period when, presumably, the bike had been treated gently.

The rear tyre, specially designed for the Gold Wing at a reputed development cost of half a million quid, is a weird 4.50 × 17 inch size which makes your choice of replacements limited. It's made by Dunlop Japan, who unfortunately do not seem to use compounds anything like good old British Dunlop rubber. The tyres feel OK in the dry, but gave me a couple of frights on damp tarmac.

Happily weight does have some compensations. Most heavy bikes seem very stable when braking, and the Wing's three discs are up to Honda's consistently high standard in that department, especially the twin plates in front. The larger single rear disc is a little insensitive, but the front brake has ample power with smoothness and sensitivity. The braking distances achieved in testing may not seem particularly good, but there's a helluva lot of momentum behind a rolling Gold Wing, and a limitation to its tyres' grip.

Apart from motorway trips I began to feel that the Wing doesn't belong on British roads, and somehow, I don't think its big, brash looks belong here either. The bulbous styling reminds me of those jellymould American sedans of the Forties and early Fifties. Some people are overawed by the sheer immensity and the gadgetry, some might even find its styling appealing in a weird sort of way ('God, it's so ugly it's *beautiful*' was the reaction of one guy, not a biker, when he first saw it).

The bulging, pregnant flanks, the tasteless slab of plastic and steel forming the dummy tank, the silly spoilers each side of the radiator and the nasty bit of chromed tin screwed to the silencer all offend against my aesthetic sensibilities.

Could it be portentous that Joe Lucas lights the way for the Gold Wing, with one of

Same tank shape wears a different paint treatment, the saddle acquires some chrome trim, and we're back to the four chromed mufflers. Whatever people may have thought about the styling of the first Wing, nobody could accuse Honda of having rushed into it without exploring a few alternatives first . . .

his fine Halogen lamps? The Japs might have our bike industry in a tight corner, but By Jove, we can still show them how to make a good headlamp.

And while we're into the electricals, a bitch about that infuriating audible warning on the indicators that causes endless embarrassment by bleeping away idiotically in time with the flashers. I got so paranoid about motorists and pedestrians staring at me, that I searched fruitlessly for a wiring snap connector to rip apart and silence the thing.

That sort of gizmo I can well do without, and the gimmicky approach to motorcycle design, as represented by the Gold Wing, leaves me cold, as you may have realised by now. The motor did impress me with its power and smoothness, but once the novelty wears off, the Gold Wing does not stand out as a memborable bike to ride. I can think of several bikes weighing half as much, giving half the power and costing half the price, which are more fun to ride than the Wing. And when it comes down to it, that's what a bike's all about—having fun. And if all the gadgets and gizmos and complexity don't make the Gold Wing any more fun, what's the point?

In the traditional world of British motorcycle journalism, where criticism of a road-test machine was often implied rather than stated categorically in 10 pt Plantin medium, reaction was swift and strong. Honda (UK) immediately cancelled all advertising with *Bike*. Sticking by its journalistic principles cost *Bike* dearly at a time when Honda was being fairly generous with its four-colour double-page spreads in other magazines. With a dominant share of the market in Britain, Honda's advertising spend was a significant part of any magazine's income. The ban was to stay in force for over a year. And with it came a refusal by Honda to supply road-test motorcycles to *Bike*; from then on, the magazine had to rely on certain dealers if they wanted to test a Honda.

The test caused a lot of debate among riders in general, too. One Wing owner told me, much later: 'If I could have got hold of Bill Haylock I'd have throttled him!' On balance, though, Haylock's test was a well-written and well-

Another variation on the theme—the distinctive black mufflers are chrome-plated and for the first time the dummy tank has a locking lid

argued piece which pointed out a lot of the Wing's shortcomings and made a few shrewd observations about the bike, Honda's philosophy and future trends in motorcycling. He was right that the Wing was conventional rather than revolutionary; right that it was 'an image bike' (and, boy, what an image bike it was going to become) but wrong to say that it was a *pure* image bike without any functional intent; right about the poor riding position, and about the poor touring range. He was even right about Honda trying to 'turn bikers into socially acceptable two-wheeled motorists'. If Honda were to concentrate solely on producing rip-snorting road-burners for the filthy denim brigades of the Western world they would never achieve sufficient volume sales, profits or growth.

But Bill Haylock's basic mistake was to lose total objectivity in his over-reaction to a motorcycle that was as different from his own personal tastes as chalk is to cheese. His own motorcycle at that time was a 450 cc Ducati Desmo: a loud, poorly finished, unreliable, highly specialized sportster with amazing handling and roadholding and good performance for its size. The 450 Desmo was great for letting it all hang out on twisty back roads but would be nowhere near most riders' list of prime candidates for a two-week, 3000-mile international tour.

If Haylock's personal view was that motorcyclists should not be socially acceptable two-wheeled motorists then that should not have intruded into an objective evaluation of a new motorcycle, in my opinion. Furthermore, his objection 'to a manufacturer deciding that he'll design what he thinks I ought to have rather than what I want' was totally without foundation on two counts. First, Honda produced the Gold Wing because its market research showed that this was what a section of the motorcycle-buying public *did* want. And secondly, Honda at that time produced another 60 motorcycle models which did not resemble the Gold Wing in form or function and some of which stood a

Artist's impression shows the styling treatment taking its final shape. Maybe it's because this is closer to the bike we all know, but it certainly looks better than most of the other styling options

chance of providing the kind of riding enjoyment that Haylock sought. How stupid it would have sounded had I, in road-testing the 450 Desmo Ducati, attacked the manufacturer for having he audacity to make the kind of bike he though I ought to have rather than the kind of bike I wanted!

Two-wheeled car? In a sense, that is precisely what the Gold Wing was and is. Until the arrival of the Wing, there were precious few two-wheeled vehicles that could carry a traveller over long distances across a continent and back without requiring some kind of remedial surgery *en route*. That was the one car-like feature that the serious touring rider wanted most of all. Taking the analogy a stage further, many American Gold Wing riders see their machine as a two-wheeled Cadillac and are more than a little flattered by the association.

How was this kind of criticism received by the designers back in Japan? The Japanese motorcycle press, never critical in road tests by Western standards, generally give a warm reception to every new model, so media criticism is not something to which Honda's designers—or those in any of the other companies—are often exposed. It is often months before road tests in overseas markets are translated into Japanese and find their way back to the designers. When they do, they often go unread. When they are read, they are not taken very seriously. Certainly, the Gold Wing design team was not especially interested in what the world's press had to say about their creation, good or bad. They had set out to build the King of Motorcycles and that, in their view, was simply what they had done.

In any event, not every tester reacted so strongly against their new creation. Contrast that GL1000 K1 test from *Bike* with the following K2 test from *Motorcyclist Illustrated*.

It was gone midnight. Over 350 miles had passed beneath my wheels that mild September evening, but as I eased the Gold Wing off the A2 near my Gravesend home I toyed with the idea of pressing on to Dover, catching some improbable late-night

Even in 1974, Honda was planning a fully equipped touring version of the Wing—an early Interstate, if you like. The saddlebags are Krauser, the fairing a Windjammer—a combination which ironically became extremely popular with many Wing Nuts

ferry to France, and riding east to meet the sunrise. Few bikes drive me to such levels of fantasy at that time of the morning in the autumn, but the fact that I resisted temptation due more to the lack of a suitably-timed ferry than rider fatigue says an awful lot for the big Honda's credentials as a serious touring motorcycle.

For a start the machine's large, bright halogen headlight with its excellent light pattern on both main and dipped beams, was putting out enough light in the right places for it to matter little that the sun had migrated to the other side of the world. And that's more than can be said for most bikes; the Gold Wing's headlight has but one or two peers in the motorcycle world.

Then there's the suspension, the seat and riding position. All three are not remotely in the BMW class but by Japanese standards there is little to moan about from the comfort angle. The suspension is well damped at the front end considering the machine's formidable weight at 635 lb, but gives slightly too harsh a ride for a luxury tourer. The rear shock absorbers are five-way adjustable and in the softer positions return a fairly comfortable ride. Their damping was just about adequate but might be improved upon by fitting S & W or Girling units; if the bike were mine I would leave them alone. The dualseat turned out to be surprisingly comfortable. I felt no unwelcome twinges after a 350-mile day, and while the Americans seem to have a vast array of after-market perches for the Wing I'd be quite happy to keep the stock item. The pillion portion must be very comfortable: my wife fell asleep on one cross-London trip!

The riding position was another example of the same old Oriental failing: great up to about 85 mph, but beyond that speed it's too upright. The footrests are in the right place for my taste, but the handlebar could stand being flatter to accommodate the forward-leaning stance we all know and love. But given the constraints on high-speed travel imposed by our masters in Whitehall, my progress on the night in question was

All the development work paid off with the launch of the GL1000 at the Cologne Motorcycle Show in October 1974. In the climate of the performance-orientated mid-seventies, most people were impressed; some dismissed the GL as a two-wheeled car

not unduly impeded by wind pressure.

And then there's the engine. The watercooled flat four may appear to traditionalists to be the antithesis of what motorcycling is all about, but it's this very motor that gives the Gold Wing real character. Whereas most in-line fours now seem bland and unappealing despite their highly creditable performance, the Wing's horizontally opposed four cylinders produce the kind of power delivery that places the machine in a category all its own.

The exceptionally light twistgrip feels like it is attached to the carburettors by power-assisted hydraulics rather than twin cables. The motor's response to the throttle is so fluid, particularly in the mid-range but essentially throughout the 8500 rpm power band, that the power flows to the back wheel with an effortless surge which makes high-gear acceleration an incomparable pleasure. Other bikes might beat the Honda in a fifth-gear throttle roll-on comparison, but the way the Wing picks you up and pushes you progressively towards the horizon is a rare and endearing feature. With 80 bhp on hand the Honda loses none of this ability when laden with passenger and baggage. The only thing to watch here is the gross vehicle weight rating: with a couple of well-built adults aboard you are limited to perhaps 30 lb of luggage if the factory recommendations are followed.

This smooth transition of combustion power into forward motion had made my journey one of the least tiring in my experience. The almost total absence of noise

Four 32 mm Keihin constant-velocity butterfly-throttle carburettors fed the four cylinders of the original Gold Wing. Throttle response was so silky smooth that the connection might have been by hydraulics rather than cable

above 50 mph also contributed to my comfort, as the water jacketing keeps mechanical sound down to a clicking from the tappets which is soon lost in the breeze. The exhaust too is well silenced, yet emits an authoritative growl when accelerating hard from a standstill. Sitting there with only the wind for accompaniment, my ears free from mechanical assault, body enjoying the complete lack of vibration and my senses revelling in the engine's responsiveness, perhaps you will begin to understand why I just wanted to keep on riding.

Not that everything in the garden is rosy—it isn't. It's just that with the Gold Wing (I was testing the latest K2 version with minor modifications over the original Wing; a K3 model with further mods is available in the States but won't hit the UK market until the end of 1978) Honda have the main ingredients for a good touring bike just right. Perhaps next year's K3 will be even nearer the ideal.

The one area that must be sorted out before long is ultra-high-speed straight-line stability. Up to 100 mph the machine sits there on the road with all the stability one would expect of a heavyweight. Side draughts from overtaken artics pass unnoticed, and even strong sidewinds have less effect than on some other big bikes. But at 100 mph and over, on that longitudinally ribbed concrete surface which crops up on many roads, the test machine would break into a disconcerting and often downright frightening weave without provocation from raised white lines or cats' eyes. This weave seemed to stem from the rear end, and I feel the 4.50 section rear tyre is to blame. The Honda 750 K7 sports the same rubberwear and exhibited the selfsame tendencies

The electric fuel gauge (*right*) was something I hadn't seen on a motorcycle before. Honda made the mistake of placing it just where most touring riders would strap a tank bag. The fact that the gauge was highly inaccurate made the positioning a moot point, anyway

The very concept of a glove compartment (*opposite page*) on a motorcycle merely confirmed the worst fears of those who derided the Wing as a two-wheeled car. Lifting the tool tray revealed the air cleaner. The compartment was really too small to be useful. And tank-top bags had to come right off to get at the fuel cap on tour. Fuel drain tray to catch spills was neat, though

on the same surface. After slowing down, moving back along the seat, crouching low and gripping the handlebar much more tightly the same speed could be attained on the same surface without the weave, but crossing raised white lines when changing lanes brought on the condition once more. Replacement tyres could make a big difference, which is a pity because otherwise these tyres work well. They give plenty of cornering traction, and are acceptable in wet weather.

Owners thinking of changing tyres will be pleased to know that whatever covers Dunlop is dreaming up for this model, they must be good. The test bike was collected the same day it was returned by Dunlop's tyre testers, and they had worn away the ends of both footrests as well as a sizeable portion of the left leg of the centre stand. After this treatment there was no way I could ground the stand on public roads, and the bike had to be heeled way over before the footrests touched down. New Wings that have not had the benefit of the Dunlop testers' treatment may ground the little nubs on the footrest ends more readily, but even then ground clearance is adequate.

The Honda's ability to be thrown around on twisty lanes surprised me. It needed a firm hand when laying it into a tight corner, but considering its weight and sheer bulk the Wing performed creditably in an area for which it was obviously not specifically designed. The motor's useful spread of torque and the duplex frame's acceptable handling allowed high average speeds over sinuous stretches of road.

Braking was just so-so. The triple discs never gave cause for concern, but they offered the rider little feedback and required strong pressure from high speed. The large rear disc did not seem exceptionally powerful, but all three worked acceptably in the wet, again much to my surprise. Preliminary results of tests by the Transport and Road Research Laboratory into disc brake materials show no difference in wet-weather performance between stainless steel, chrome, and cast iron discs, either drilled or undrilled. It appears the problem is more one of water retention by the pads, and the

Fold-down panels on sides of the dummy tank were all part of the Gold Wing image. They offered easy access to main electrical components. The right-side cover housed emergency kickstart lever, subsequently dropped

delay we all despise on many Japanese bikes is caused by the pads not heating up sufficiently to dry out quickly. The final test results from the TRRL should make interesting reading.

The transition from the early Gold Wing to the new K2 has also meant a price increase from a highly competitive £1,600 to a still cheap-at-the-price £1,995. The only visual difference is a more tasteful paint job and chrome covers on the black exhaust header pipes. The factory may have breathed slightly on the engine as Honda engineers are wont to do between model years, but nothing is substantially different. The top speed of 118 mph for a rider weighing 14 stone, crouching down in a two-piece rainsuit, could probably be improved upon, but there seems little point. I am sure about 123–124 mph is possible, but since the disturbing weave reared its head during my top speed runs my mind was not entirely wrapped up in eking out those last few mph.

Sitting upright, a gradient and a headwind combined to slow the Honda to 90 mph in top gear, yet on many smaller bikes I would have been changing down a cog or two to maintain 70 mph.

The standard of finish is very good, especially the quality of the chrome plating. The engine is well finished and is fairly easy to keep clean. As one would expect from Japan, convenience plays an important part in the overall design. The plugs and their caps are readily accessible; an oil level sight window on the right of the engine told me the bike had used no oil in 1000 miles of testing; the sidestand has a rubber flap to effectively take care of stand retraction for the careless among us; and the centre stand is not too awkward, bearing in mind the size and weight of the Wing. The mirrors are better than the Honda average—they are smooth throughout and you can actually see beyond your elbows. Like the throttle, the clutch action is very light and the five-speed gearbox shifts easily and cleanly. The dipswitch was the only awkward control, being a bit of a

Double-disc front brake was powerful, but the weight of the Wing caused some fork flex under heavy braking. The stanchion diameter was later increased by 2 mm to 39 mm on the GL1100. Polished alloy rims were a nice touch, just before the ComStar era

stretch and badly placed. And the horn is quite inadequate—it's almost embarrassing to use.

Perhaps the best-known feature of the Gold Wing is its dummy tank which comprises three panels; these open to reveal the electrics and fuses on the left, the radiator header tank and stowaway kickstart crank on the right, and a toolkit and glove box in the centre. The tools are above average, and beneath the tool tray lies the air cleaner for easy servicing. For some unaccountable reason the radiator header needed topping up twice during the test, although no leaks showed up and the automatic fan behind the radiator never came into play. I understand that the hose clips may be the cause of coolant loss—it's worth checking. The water temperature gauge, mounted in the tachometer, registered just on the cool side of 'normal' throughout the test.

The real petrol tank nestles under the seat, out of harm's way and helping to lower the centre of gravity. The only drawback is that it holds a mere four gallons, and while five would be more practical an owner will find it virtually impossible to fit a larger tank at a reasonable cost; Honda ought to do the job properly and fit a five-gallon tank as standard. However the fuel consumption averaged out at exactly 40 mpg, good for 160 miles on a tankful which, although way behind a BMW's 200-plus, is on a par with much of the competition. The only *faux pas* is in the positioning of the electric fuel gauge—sitting there in the middle of that fake tank, it is more than likely to be covered by a tank bag when the Wing s used for its intended purpose. Never mind—the gauge

Shaft drive was one of the main attractions. Until the Wing came along, you either adjusted and lubed the final drive chain daily on tour, or you paid dearly for a BMW. Honda later fitted a grease nipple which put an end to stripping the drive unit for greasing

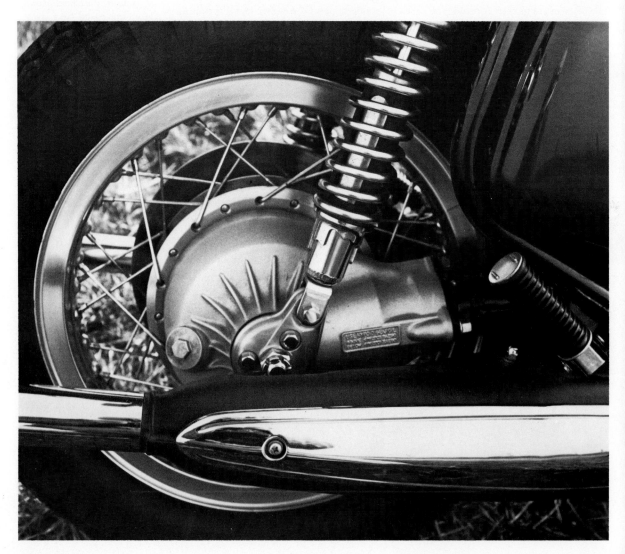

was so inaccurate on the test bike it registered empty when the tank was almost half full!

The engine is a fairly straightforward 999 cc flat four, with single overhead camshafts driven by toothed belt from the crankshaft. One 32 mm carb feeds each of the cylinders, and the traditional torque reaction of a horizontally opposed engine with crankshaft mounted longitudinally is countered by a contra-rotating flywheel. Unlike the BMs, the Honda does not lean to the right when the throttle is blipped. Primary drive is by Morse Hyt-Vo chain. Riding the Wing, a slight roughness can be felt below 4000 rpm if the throttle is snapped open in fourth or fifth gears, but this is only relative to the utter smoothness of the engine and transmission at all other times. The package is rounded off by the immense attraction of shaft drive.

The engine's flexibility and smoothness, coupled with light low-speed steering, makes the Wing one of the easier bikes to ride in city traffic. Giving the normal run of more town-orientated two-wheeled commuters the slip in the rush hour is one of the memories I cherish, purely because it seems so unlikely. And yet out on the open road the machine is turning over at a leisurely 6000 rpm in top at 100 mph. It could—and indeed bloody well should, at the price—handle better and exhibit more straight-line stability at speed. But even with these present limitations, the GL1000 K2 captured my imagination as a desirable and effortless tourer. It just begs to be ridden across a continent, and the next time the opportunity arises I think I'll succumb to that

The rear disc brake on early Wings was powerful enough but felt wooden in operation. Many riders moaned about the rear shocks and changed them for Girlings, Konis, S&Ws and other brands in a search for a better ride

temptation. This time round I let the head rule the heart: I parked the Wing and went to bed.

It embarrasses me to admit to being the writer of that test: not because I disagree now in the slightest with its tone but because I went on record as pronouncing the dualseat comfortable, the shocks acceptable and the front forks well damped! It was so long ago now that I can no longer recall whether I was lucky with that particular Wing, or easy to please, or just plain wrong on a couple of points! What I do remember is the excellent ground clearance afforded by the metal-wearing efforts of the Dunlop tyre testers, and the fact that despite popular opinion I found I could go quite fast through the twisties by concentrating and working hard at it. Maybe I was more reckless or less imaginative in those days. . . . But the contrast in the two tests is an important one. Here was one tester who had time for only one set of motorcycling rules and who condemned a new bike because it fell so far outside them, and another tester who found so much sheer 'great to be out on the road' riding pleasure in the Gold Wing that he was prepared to forgive it many of its weak points. I

Typical of Honda was the neat packaging of the electrics behind the dummy tank side. A lot of riders wished Honda had put as much thought into providing better fuel capacity in the under-seat tank

would submit that the latter approach is one that would find favour with Wing owners worldwide. But it is also a fact that *Bike* had a circulation some four times greater than that of *Motorcyclist Illustrated* and that this may in part account for the Wing's lack of initial acceptance in the British market.

3 Success in America

While controversy raged in Europe, the American motorcycle press and the touring fraternity were taking the Wing to their hearts.

Cycle was first to test the new arrival from Japan and first to sing its praises. In an eight-page analysis and road-test, the top-selling monthly motorcycle magazine found little to criticise and much to appreciate. 'If Honda is going to sell a motorcycle for $3000, then by all that's holy it's going to be worth it,' ran the subhead. 'For your dough you get a shaft drive bonus, a triple-disc bonus, a fat rear tire bonus, enough indicator lights to trim a Christmas tree and that final, unexpected, transcendent Extra: except for the Kawasaki 903 Z-1, the GL-1000 is the hardest-accelerating 1975 production motorcycle you can buy.'

That performance came as a surprise to many. As *Cycle* said, when the Gold Wing was introduced at a dealer convention in Las Vegas, 'it was assumed by most that the Gold Wing was a soft, posh and mildly-tuned straight-line tourer. Most were wrong.' *Cycle* went on to prove just *how* wrong with a

This was about the most conservatively modified Wing at Wing Ding '82 in Colorado. It's a 1975 with sensible mods like simple screen, saddlebags, seat, shocks, exhaust and front fender. Compared to most Wings, this one is box stock!

blistering standing quarter-mile time of 12.92 seconds at 104.52 mph—
nothing to write home about these days, but incredibly quick by the standards
of 1975. The results surprised everyone—including the testers: 'We knew that
the bike was fast, but a trip to the drag strip astonished everyone. Bringing the
revs up to 8000 and dumping the clutch produced a tire-howling smoke-
thrower that lasted a good 150 feet. Times and speeds improved for four runs,
with the best being 13.00 seconds at 102.38 mph. On the fourth run the clutch
was slipped to prevent tire-spin, and promptly scorched itself into uselessness.
Back at Honda, the engine was removed and the clutch plates were replaced
with ones introduced to the production line after our pilot production test
bike.' A return trip to the strip with the new clutch produced the second fastest
time in production motorcycle quarter-miling.

That fact alone was enough to guarantee the Wing a measure of instant sales
in the United States. In the euphoria of motorcycling's mid-70s heyday,
quarter-mile times and outright top speeds were factors that weighed heavily in
the minds of superbike buyers. That philosophy was reflected a year or two
earlier when one of the leading American magazines ran a 750 comparison test
based on a compendium of variables including acceleration, braking, lap times
around a racing circuit and one or two other items. The winner, and therefore
the 'best 750 on the market', was the Kawasaki 750 two-stroke triple. It had
won because its accelerative performance more than outweighed its handling
deficiencies and produced not only the best quarter-mile time but also, if I
recall correctly, the fastest lap time on the track. Today, few of us remember
the big triple as anything other than a devastatingly quick flash in the pan with
abysmal handling, appalling fuel economy and a tendency to sound clapped-
out after a year's hard riding.

The Wing's early sales success, however, was boosted not only by its engine
performance and its much-acclaimed smoothness and refinement. The
majority of American riders—and touring riders in particular—may not be
quite so fussy about handling and roadholding as their European counterparts
profess to be, but a *Bike*-style panning of the Wing's handling abilities would
not have helped sales any. *Cycle* gave the Wing a clean bill of health in this area:
'After the 500-mile service checks were done we began to lean on the engine a
little harder and drag things going around corners on our favourite deserted
roads. The footrests have steel feelers on their ends that are designed to touch
the ground before the stands or mufflers hang up. With the shock absorber
springs set full-soft for freeway cruising, the footrests drag quite easily during
moderately quick rides on twisting roads. A special wrench in the tool kit
adjusts the spring-load for hard cornering during sporty rides or when carrying
a passenger. With the springs wound up tight the bike may be ridden very hard
without anything grounding.

'The GL's low center of gravity gives it an extremely responsive feel for a
machine that weighs close to 650 pounds. The only time the rider notices the
difference in feel from one of the 750s, which weigh about 125 pounds less, is
when the big bike is muscled through a series of tight switchback turns.
Neither end of the GL oscillates or snakes around alarmingly within the
bounds of the bike's ground clearance. The only thing some of our staff
members complained about during frequent on- and off-throttle spurts was
the lurch caused by gear slack in the first four speeds.

'Both front and rear brakes function perfectly. They will haul the massive
GL down from highly illegal rates to sedate crawls in incredibly and repeatably
short distances.'

Next page This
immaculately customised
GL1100 and matching
trailer waits with
hundreds of others for the
start of the Poker Run at
Wing Ding '82 in
Steamboat Springs.
Minutes later, the heavens
opened but everyone kept
on riding, chrome-plate
notwithstanding

Cycle's analysis of the new tourer highlighted only a few flaws: a mediocre ride over the expansion joints of Los Angeles freeways and a poor handlebar/seat/footrest relationship that was too cramped for tall riders. Otherwise, 'long cruises on the Gold Wing were something we looked forward to. You don't have to mess with the chain every time you stop for gas. In fact, you don't have to do anything but stop for gas and enjoy the trip'. Those attributes found favour immediately with the American motorcycling public in sufficient quantity to ensure the sale of 4000 Gold Wings in the first year. And Honda has been selling up to 25,000 Wings a year there ever since.

Reading a road test and buying a motorcycle on the strength of it is one thing: agreeing afterwards that you did the right thing is entirely another. But within 18 months of the Wing hitting US roads for the first time, the touring

Frame-welding at Honda of America Manufacturing Inc. in Maryville, Ohio, where Gold Wings have been manufactured since 1980

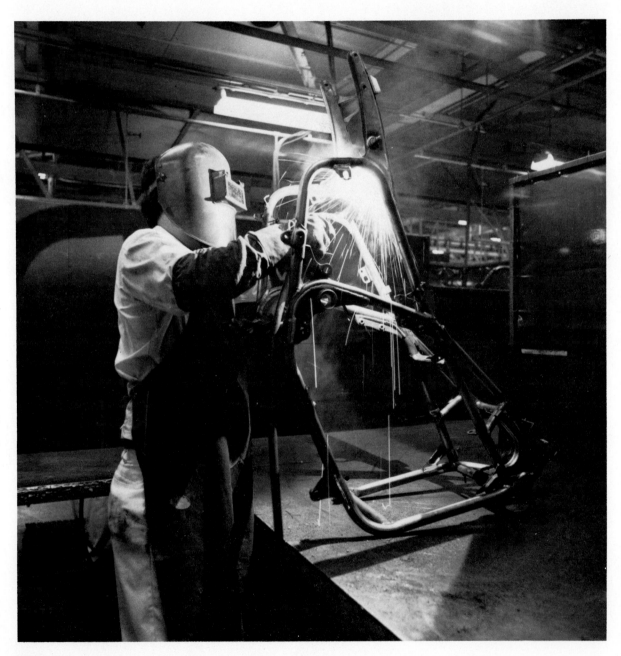

magazine *Road Rider* asked its Wing-owning readers to report on their time with the GL1000. A total of 582 owners responded. On average, they had owned their Wings for 1.2 years and 9500 miles. They rated smoothness and quietness as the best features, but had some harsh words to say about suspension compliance, seat comfort, riding position and—albeit to a lesser degree—handling. But 25.4 per cent of owners rated the Wing as 'excellent' and another 46.1 per cent 'good', with 12 per cent rating it as 'fair' and only 11 per cent as 'poor'. The rest didn't offer an opinion.

Even in those early days, several owners had notched up more than 50,000 miles on their Wings. The 11 per cent who rated 'reliability' as its best feature had averaged more than 26,500 miles each. 'There is no question,' *Road Rider* concluded, 'that the Gold Wing owners are out there riding their machines and making their odometers work hard. When all is said and done, this concept of 'usability' is probably the single most pertinent reason for the Gold Wing's instant success—and for the reciprocal zeal of the people who own them. The machine was tailor-made for the type of riding American touring riders do most.'

The magazine left it to reader Allen Ivinx of Daytona Beach, Florida, to sum up thus: 'I have ridden motorcycles for my transportation since 1947. Never have so many good features been incorporated into one machine with so little compromise. For a touring machine this has to be the closest machine to hitting the market right on the bullseye. This is the best bike in the touring class for any sum of money.'

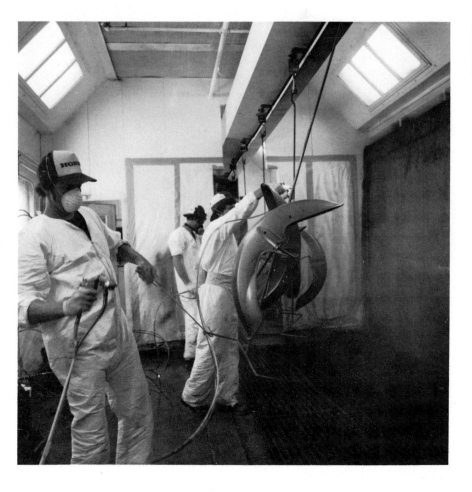

Gold Wing fenders glide through the spray booth at Honda's Maryville production plant

He was echoing the feelings of thousands of American touring riders; the Wing continued to sell well in the United States aided by its specification and continuing good press reviews. *Motor Cycle World* in November 1976 dubbed the Gold Wing as 'a comfortable, long distance touring machine with little, if anything, in its class that can match its capacity to devour huge strands of black asphalt spaghetti without so much as a hiccup'.

As the years progressed and newer competitors like the Yamaha XS750 and XS1100, Suzuki GS850 and GS1000, Harley-Davidson FLT, BMW R100RT, and Kawasaki KZ1000 and KZ1300 entered the market, Wing sales continued to hold up well, aided by frequent updates. The press still rated the machine highly. In March 1978, *Cycle* called the new GL1000 'king smoothie' and paid tribute to the success of the Wing in the US: 'Head out on an open road in good weather and you'll see Honda GL1000 Gold Wings . . . everywhere. Since the introduction of the Gold Wing in 1975, touring riders have embraced the Gold Wing like no other relatively-new motorcycle. It's easy to see why—the Gold Wing has solid credentials for long-haul riding. It's smooth, quiet, reliable, shaft-driven and able to carry a big load.'

But *Cycle*, objective as ever, also pointed out that even with its many improvements for 1978, the Wing now ranked behind the Yamaha XS1100 as a long-distance bike 'in its fundamental touring elements. That should surprise no one,' said the magazine. 'In its heart and soul the GL1000 still says 1975. The XS11 rings 1978. And time waits for no machine, not even the Gold

Interstate fairings and luggage equipment are checked for flaws at Maryville before joining the main production line

Wing.' With shrewd perception, *Cycle* commented that Honda had the luxury of continuing to reshape the Gold Wing for touring-use only while developing the six-cylinder CBX to cater to the go-faster market. Yamaha, on the other hand, had only the XS1100 for both market segments.

And that is precisely how the scenario developed. But before Honda had the chance to jump ahead of the rest once more with the launch of the 1100, the GL1000 continued to lose ground in the eyes of some testers. In a major six-bike touring comparison in June 1979, the American magazine *Motorcyclist* rated the Honda as a 'loser' on the grounds of poor ride comfort, excessive weight, poor handling, poor throttle response and peaky powerband. 'The Honda is more expensive than the XS1100 and does virtually nothing as well,' said *Motorcyclist*. Another loser in the comparison was the newly introduced BMW R100RT, the newest and most prestigious tourer ever from the German

Fairings meet Interstates on the assembly line at Maryville. At last, the all-American tourer is made in America

firm. I rode one of the new BMWs in February that year and toured with it and was enormously impressed. The model they tested was full of faults; mine was not. Once again, and not for the last time in road-testing, the peculiarities of the test bike and the tester's personal preferences took their toll.

The winners in the comparison were the XS1100 and Suzuki's new GS850, while Kawasaki's new KZ1000ST and KZ1300 were rated as 'in the hunt' and better than both the BMW and the Wing. On the face of it, the newer motorcycles had many advantages over the Gold Wing by virtue of their later design and the rate of technical progress within the motorcycle industry in the late 1970s. But the BMW and the Wing sold well in America in 1979, not least because a lot of touring riders are more concerned about how a bike feels out there on the highway than with some of the criteria used by road-testers.

But the grass wasn't exactly peeping out from under the sneakers in Wako all

An Interstate is put through its paces on a rolling road before crating and shipping. Note the external battery by the rear wheel

this time, and in 1980 Honda hit back with the enlarged and much improved and updated GL1100. The extent of the internal and external changes is dealt with in Chapter 8. The important differences (air suspension, redesigned engine, better seat, new frame and many others) added up to a whole new motorcycle that retained the old qualities which had endeared the GL1000 to about 220,000 riders already. Here, in one fell swoop, were the answers to criticisms that had been around and building since 1975. And, by offering for the first time a fully equipped touring version called the Interstate, Honda was selling precisely the sort of touring bike that many people believed the Wing should have been right from the start. The press loved it, and so did the American touring public, and for the first time the Wing really began to take off in a big way in Europe also, with 20,000 sales in the US and 5000 in Europe.

In May 1980, *Cycle World* ran a six-bike comparison between the new GL1100 Interstate, BMW R100T, Harley-Davidson FLT-80, Kawasaki KZ1000, Suzuki GS850 and Yamaha XS1100. This was virtually the same six fielded by *Motorcyclist* 11 months earlier; what a difference a year makes! This time the Gold Wing beat the lot! 'That super suspension, combined with the bike's absolute troublefree nature and lack of serious vices make it the highway favourite of the test,' said the editors. 'Every test rider but one chose the Honda as the bike for a cross-country jaunt.' They still criticized the seat, the riding position, touring range and, in the case of the test model, indifferent performance. Everybody that year hated the crash bars because they bruised the rider's shins virtually every time he put his feet down; Honda, wisely, changed 'em for 1982.

Cycle caught up with the Interstate in September 1981 and echoed the general praise for the revised Wing: 'The Gold Wing has at last achieved the kind of ride compliance expected in contemporary touring-bike circles.' Exit long-standing gripe number one. 'The seat is marvellously supple. All our testers appreciated its softness and well-contoured shape. For the record, Honda subtly recontoured the 1981 Gold Wing's seat, getting it lower and more in tune with the American backside.' Exit long-standing gripe number two. The Gold Wing was finally coming of age.

But it was in 1982 that Honda drew the most prolific praise for the Gold Wing with the introduction of the Aspencade. Again, the differences in specification that make up the Aspencade are covered fully in Chapter 8. Once more Honda had blitzed the opposition by offering for sale the most fully equipped and thoughtfully detailed touring motorcycle ever. And again, *Cycle* led the cheerleaders: 'Honda just doesn't let up. Year after year, the company updates the Gold Wing and keeps it about four steps ahead of the competition. For 1983, the Aspencade, Interstate Cruiser Supreme, has a variety of innovative refinements which help it maintain its status as king of the road.' Just as the 1975 Gold Wing had brought together in one package for the first time a number of features seen previously on disparate motorcycles, so too the 1983 Aspencade offered in a single motorcycle such innovations as interconnected front/rear brakes, brake-sensitive anti-dive air suspension with push-button adjustment and LCD instrumentation.

'The many changes for 1983 reflect Honda's attitude about the Gold Wing,' said the magazine. 'The refinements are innovative, somewhat trendy, basically functional, and all in all make the Aspencade an even better touring bike than before. It is, still, the class of the field by far.'

Perhaps most telling of all, the 1983 Aspencade even found favour with the same magazine which had rubbished the original Gold Wing back in 1975—

that's right, *Bike*. Editor Brecon Quaddy took an Aspencade on a tour of Continental Europe in the company of a BMW R100RS and a Laverda 1000RGS. His first surprise came when he left home too late to catch the 10.00 pm car ferry from Southampton: 'Ya, boo and sucks to everyone (including me) who thought Aspencades weren't included in the category of motorcycles built to go places fast. It covered the distance (85 miles) in 70 minutes and they were still loading lorries on to the ferry when we arrived.'

Over the next couple of thousand miles he found cause to praise the Wing's engine performance, its handling (within limits), fuel economy, braking, and comfort. The conclusion? 'In all, the Honda acquitted itself remarkably well as a Eurotripper, considering its origins as a Yank interstate roller. Quicker and more agile than its size and weight would suggest, it also turned out to be more frugal than its European rivals, not to mention the most comfortable as far as passengers are concerned. Air suspension that really works is great when the fiddly business of setting it up is done for you by an electric pump and a couple of push buttons. Pose value apart, the GL1100A is nonetheless a serious tourer. It may look like an elephant but it will fly if you want it to.' Funny what eight years of development and a change of road-tester can do for a bike!

I doubt if the Gold Wing, even in its latest incarnation, will ever please all of the testers all of the time. The 1983 Aspencade drew wondrous praise from *Cycle* and other American magazines; it even managed to gain acceptance and outright approval from *Bike* in Britain; and yet the same model was put down in no uncertain terms by *Bike Australia* for its single-minded commitment to

Honda's 258,000 ft^2 factory in Maryville, Ohio, was opened in June 1979 with a production capacity of 60,000 motorcycles a year. Manufacturing began with the Elsinore CR250R in 1979. The CBX1000 followed in November that year and Gold Wing production started in 1980

highway touring at the expense of other forms of riding. 'Two up, with a moderate amount of luggage, this bike cannot be taken around corners properly, unless you happen to be into scraping at every opportunity,' said tester Peter Thoeming. But Peter, as fair as the day is long, admitted to having enjoyed his weekend on the Aspencade and recommended the Wing for the touring rider who could afford the luxury of a specialized touring motorcycle.

Ultimately, after the testers have ridden the bikes, made their measurements and compared notes with competitive machinery, the final say on whether a motorcycle is good, bad or indifferent rests with you and me. We vote with our wallets and our cheque books. And through good years and bad, rave reviews and hatchet-jobs, Honda has been selling consistently 25,000 Gold Wings a year. That's the real measure of its value and its success.

4 The riders

According to a survey carried out by *Road Rider* magazine in the United States in 1976, the average Wing rider was 40.8 years old, had been riding for 12.9 years and rode an average of 11,500 miles each year. Those raw facts, published in January 1977, are now some eight years out of date. If the same survey were to be conducted today, we'd probably find that virtually all the original respondents were still riding Wings, that the average had crept up to at least 45 and that the years of riding experience had increased proportionately.

Just who are these Wing Nuts? They're older and more experienced as motorcyclists than the average bike rider, that's for sure. Motorcycling traditionally is a young person's pastime. Go to any motorcycle rally, club run or club night and the over-40s are the exception rather than the rule. At any Wing gathering, however, they're in the majority, ably supported by the over-50s and more than a handful of over-60s. At Wing Ding '82 in Steamboat Springs, Colorado—the annual gathering of Wing Nuts organised by the Gold Wing Road Riders Association—I met 28-year-old Ron Cronk from Van Nuys, California, and his girlfriend Cheryl Ford, also 28. I was 28 as well, and we looked around for some contemporaries to see if there might be grounds for forming a junior branch of the GWRRA. There were a few likely candidates, but not many. 'The guys in the Van Nuys Chapter (of the GWRRA) call me The Kid,' Ron said ruefully. He's 30 now and he's probably still The Kid. Down at the local Kawasaki GPz appreciation society he'd be considered over the hill.

Age is perhaps the single most distinguishing feature that differentiates the Wing lover from other motorcyclists, although BMW and Glide owners may run them close on years. The reasons are as straightforward as they are obvious. There aren't many youngsters that can lay out upwards of $8000 at current prices for a touring motorcycle—let alone the thousands of dollars most Wing Nuts spend on gilding the lily. And it takes a while for a motorcyclist to get the raw thrill of blinding acceleration and back-road high-speed scratching out of his system. The very qualities that have endeared about a quarter of a million riders the world over to the Wing have little relevance to the rider who owns a GPz550 and yearns for a VF750 Interceptor, Ducati Pantah or Laverda Montjuich. Also, while touring is by no means the sole preserve of the senile, it is still a minority pastime among riders. Younger riders who have the urge to see distant horizons tend to do so on their existing machines, however unsuitable; this is especially true in Europe. Long-distance touring consumes a lot of fuel and tyres and runs up hotel, motel or camping equipment bills. The young touring enthusiast who buys the best equipment for the job (the Wing) and all the trappings of the long-distance two-wheeled traveller may find himself or herself with no cash left for the trip.

Observation shows that Wing riders in Britain and Continental Europe are on average a shade younger than their American counterparts. The cash constraints and the preference for lighter, sharper-handling machinery are, if anything, even more true in Europe, but we don't appear to have the prepondrance of middle-aged Wing-mounted couples that characterises the US scene. Most American Wing Nuts are middle-class professionals, retired professional people and retired farmers.

Paul Hildebrand, National Director of the Gold Wing Road Riders Association, says that Gold Wing riders in the US 'represent a segment of upper-middle-class America. The typical Wing rider holds a managerial or white-collar position and is in his or her 40s'. Looking around at the riders attending Wing Ding '82 I'd say that was a fairly accurate analysis and one that translates reasonably well to the European situation. In Europe, though, there is a greater proportion of younger Wing owners and, in Britain at least, the riders span the working and middle classes. 'Upper middle class' riders are the

If you're gonna travel, do it in style: this couple rolling into Wing Ding at Steamboat Springs didn't forget essentials like the trailer-mounted ice chest

exception rather than the rule. It's really more a question of how you define the social structure: the same types of people ride Wings on both sides of the Atlantic.

'A lot of older people nearing retirement buy the Wing as a toy,' says Larry Tietz of Honda R&D. 'To most of them it's more than just a nice motorcycle—it's a hobby, an attempt to recapture their lost youth. Their kids are grown up and the parents have the money to do something they couldn't afford to do when they were younger: buy a really first-class motorcycle to tour the country. For many older Wing Nuts it's a chance to do something they always wanted to but which *their* parents would never have allowed.'

Phil Jacks, who rides an '81 Wing and hails from Pinewood, Colorado, describes the Gold Wing as 'an ideal Mom and Pop bike. Many older riders choose the Wing as their first-ever motorcycle simply because they like the way it looks.'

Whatever their age, Wing Nuts are quite clear as to why they bought their flat fours. Walter Knapp of Albuquerque, New Mexico, spoke for a lot of riders when he summed up: 'Honda made a $500 engine and put it in a $50 suspension system.' Not everyone would go quite as far as Walter did to remedy the situation: he shoehorned a GL engine into a Harley Electra Glide frame, added a front end from a 1980 FLT, a Harley fender, Monroe shocks and all the Glide touring accessories. But most riders agree that the Gold Wing gave the touring motorcyclist the smoothest, sweetest-running, most reliable and quietest engine in the business in a package flawed by inferior suspension—until the 1980 models, at any rate.

Signing on for the Poker Run at Wing Ding. The riders are generally older than the two-wheeled norm

Doug Blackman, an American who's been riding for 27 years, calls the Wing the best-balanced bike on the market. 'It's the feeling you get when riding it that makes it special,' he says. Mike Bridge, an automotive engineer who is also chairman of the Gold Wing Owners Club of Great Britain, has been riding his 1977 K2 for nearly seven years. 'There's something about it, something different that makes everything else on two wheels just another motorcycle,' he says. A fellow club member of Mike's told me: 'I like it because it's different from all the Japanese straight fours and because it has plenty of power.'

Ron Cronk from Van Nuys likes his Wing because of its smoothness and because it 'stays put on the road—it doesn't get blown about.' Dan Cloute from Milwaukee traded his Suzuki 850 with full Vetter touring equipment for his '82 Interstate and Pal trailer. The Interstate's fairing was a major selling point which helped convince him to buy the Wing. Another American rider in his 60s was won over by the standard touring equipment on the Interstate: 'I put 70,000 miles on my CB500 four and it gave me great service and reliability. So when I wanted a touring bike I was inclined towards the Interstate. There are no problems in fitting accessories when you buy a factory-equipped touring bike. The motor works fine: it's really superb. And watercooling is a big plus. I'd buy another Wing, but Honda still has a way to go, especially with the suspension.'

Graham and Marian from Milton Keynes are on their third Wing, an Interstate (or Gold Wing De Luxe in the UK), after putting 10,000 miles on a K1 and 8000 miles on a KZ. 'I fancied a Wing from the first moment I saw one,' he says, 'but lack of money coupled with being a bit wild stopped me from

Wing Nuts browse among some of the dressers parked outside the Sheraton Hotel entrance at Steamboat Springs. As one bike pulls away from the kerb, a new one noses in. In the background is the exhibition hall

getting one. Then when I settled down and we got married I had to have one. We traded it in for a KZ because it had chrome pipes. Those K1 black pipes were terrible. I've still got a brand-new spare set which I can't sell because nobody'll have them. Anyway, we were about to deck the KZ out in Vetter touring kit when along came the Interstate which offered everything. It was cheaper to sell the KZ and buy the Interstate than to buy all the accessories for the KZ, so that's what we did.' (The K3 sold in the UK as the KZ.)

Whatever their reasons for buying their machine, Wing Nuts have earned themselves a solid reputation internationally as a friendly and responsible bunch of people. Just by being who they are and being out there on the road a lot of the time, they have been in the vanguard of the drive to improve the image of motorcycling. The very fact that the riders are older than the two-wheeled average and their bikes both glamorous and quiet has done untold good for motorcycling and helped to mend fences broken by younger riders on noisier machinery.

The problem of the behaviour of a minority of motorcyclists adversely affecting the welcome for all riders is a universal one. In Britain in recent years there has been a worrying tendency for pubs and campsites to erect 'No Motorcycles' signs based on the previous experience of the owner or manager. It's a trend that the British Motorcyclists Federation has been fighting for years and with some success. But when the Gold Wing Owners Club of Great Britain persuaded a small campsite in the scenic South-West to accommodate a group of its members the Club secretary received a letter from the Camping Club of Great Britain (which owns or sanctions a vast number of sites in Britain) saying that members of the Gold Wing Owners Club would be

In small groups of eight or ten, riders make their way out of the parking lot at the start of the Poker Run

welcome at any of its sites throughout the country.

It was this reputation that allowed the club to hold one of its annual rallies (or 'treffen' in club terminology) in the grounds of the stately home of Lord Montagu at Beaulieu near Southampton. And during the Saturday evening Lord Montagu, a British aristocrat with his own motor museum and a passion for all things automotive, brought some of his own dinner guests down to the rally site to meet the riders. He complimented club officials on everyone's behaviour, told them that the Gold Wingers were far better behaved than the rugby clubs that sometimes visit the estate, and said the Club was welcome to return at any time. You and I might think that being praised for *not* causing trouble is a pretty negative compliment, but in the real world motorcycling still has a way to go to live down its *Wild One* image completely and the Gold Wingers are doing more than their share to achieve that.

There is a certain element of conspicuous consumption and ego satisfaction among Wing Nuts. Many Wing owners couldn't care whether passers-by are even aware that they have so much money tied up in their machines. They would rightly point out that many other makes cost much more money and would say they would still own and ride a Wing if it cost half as much (they should be so lucky!) purely because it was the bike that suited their needs best.

But many more owners—perhaps a majority—are acutely aware that they are riding what is becoming one of the most expensive motorcycles on the market. They know that some observers are impressed by the sheer cash value the bike represents. And of course many of the heavily customized Wings represent investments many thousands of dollars above and beyond the basic price. More than one Wing owner has had obvious pleasure in telling me that

Against a backdrop of a ski resort out of season, riders prepare for the 1982 Wing Ding Poker Run. After days of scorching sunshine, the weather has turned decidedly British

his rig (complete with trailer) represents an investment of more than $13,000.

One can't help but admit that this degree of ostentation among grown—and, indeed, aging—adults is in large part an ego trip. GWRRA safety director Jim Cole agrees: 'Sure, the riders of the really outlandish dressers have an ego problem. But they *know* they have an ego problem and therefore it's not really a problem; it's under control.' Whichever way you look at it, you don't find many shy, retiring wallflowers riding full-dress Wings. These machines are meant to be *noticed*.

There is a touch of elitism about some Wing owners that is totally unjustified, even if one accepts that the possession of one type of car or motorcycle entitles anyone to regard himself as a member of an elite corps—and that's a debatable point. I heard one proud owner of a Wing dresser ask a young rider at a Wing rally what kind of bike he rode. The rider, whom I knew had just sold his 1000 cc BMW because of family commitments, replied that he had a CX500. 'Never mind,' said the Wing owner earnestly, patting the CX rider condescendingly on the back, 'we all had to start somewhere. I had a CX before I bought my Wing; a lot of us did. You'll progress to a Wing one day.' If he does, I hope he doesn't end up being quite so insufferable . . . .

Every motorcycle marque that has a following has its share of bores among the fans. They'll talk long and hard to anyone who'll listen about this or that aspect of their pride and joy for as long as their audience remains politely attentive. There are Gold Wing bores, too. Lots of 'em. But, even by motorcycle enthusiast standards, Wing Nuts are a particularly friendly and talkative bunch of people. They love to talk not just about Wings but about motorcycling in general and about touring in particular. Some of them like to

GWRRA National Director Paul Hildebrand gets ready to join the Poker Run. For him, the GWRRA is a full-time job. But even in the middle of Wing Ding, he makes time to go riding

get together in little groups and talk about handlebar streamers, chrome-plated fuel pump covers and ways of connecting up even more decorative lights to a mobile Christmas tree. In any event, their shared affection for the Wing and their natural affinity for togetherness led to the formation of Gold Wing owners' clubs in most countries where the Wing was introduced.

By far and away the largest of these is the Gold Wing Road Riders Association (GWRRA) which was formed in June 1977 by seven people in search of a 'family Gold Wing organisation' which would provide far better membership benefits than conventional motorcycle clubs without the usual attendant regulations. By August 1981, membership was over 6000 and growing fast, because by August 1982 it had more than doubled to 13,600 and by August 1983 it was in excess of 18,000, making the GWRRA probably the largest motorcycle club in the world. It has six full-time employees, including national director Paul Hildebrand, and is based in Phoenix, Arizona. Initial membership costs $30 and subsequent years $25. Members receive a monthly 40-page magazine, *Wing World*, a directory of members worldwide, accessory discounts, technical advice, and group accident insurance; future benefits may include a credit union, group health insurance and group motorcycle insurance. There are branches or chapters throughout the US and a very active European section to which most, if not all, of the national owners' clubs in Europe are connected, such as the Gold Wing Motor Club of Belgium, Gold Wing Club Deutschland and the Gold Wing Owners Club of Great Britain, to name but three. Other active owners' clubs exist in Holland, France, Austria, Norway, Sweden and Denmark.

The Gold Wing Owners Club of Great Britain was formed by its current

A couple of overseas Wing Nuts at a British Gold Wing Owners Club 'treffen'. The Dutch machine on the right has an LPG conversion—note the huge tank in front of the top box. It's owned by Crows Nest, one of the regulars at most European Wing rallies

Honda Gold Wing

Opposite page **The inside of these apartments at Steamboat Springs has to be seen to be believed. Yet by clubbing together with six or seven other riders, you can stay here more cheaply than in a motel**

Below **Motorcycle rallying, American-style: fashionable condominiums like these are pre-booked well in advance of Wing Ding by riders who want to be close to the centre of the action and who don't mind a little luxury**

president, Harry Ward, in May 1980 following the arrival of a 24-strong contingent of Wing Nuts from the UK at a Gold Wing rally in Belgium that March. Thirty-seven riders attended the inaugural meeting and today the club has about 1000 members. It operates one of the busiest social and riding calendars in British motorcycling and is probably the most active bike club in the UK.

The 1983 calendar kicked off with a Wing Ding (or rally) in Yorkshire in April, a London Wing Ding in May, a visit to the Dutch Treffen in May, the British Treffen in May, the Worcestershire Wing Ding, German Treffen and Scandinavian Treffen in Norway in June; July brought the GWRRA Treffen in Germany, the Three Counties Wing Ding at Malvern, Worcestershire, and the start of a two-week organized club tour of the Irish Republic; August wasn't exactly quiet with the Swiss Treffen, a Wing Ding in Chester, a treasure hunt and the Severn Wing Ding; and September brought Wing Dings in the East Midlands and at Witton Castle and the Second Gold Wing Rally at Amiens in France. That's a busy schedule by any standards, involving a lot of time in the saddle.

Each of the European owners' clubs organises its own international treffen which is attended by a contingent from each of the other Wing owners' clubs and the indefatiguable ex-paratrooper who acts as the GWRRA director in Europe, American Ray Torres. All the national clubs were out in force at the 1983 Belgian Treffen where 365 Wings were in attendance, including no fewer than 120 from the British GWOC, 84 from Germany, 58 from Holland, 52 from Belgium, and 36 from France. The Danes managed three bikes, the Swiss and Norwegians two each and the Austrians one, with seven GWRRA members making up the difference.

These international gatherings have a relaxed informality and friendliness about them which makes them more family occasions than your run-of-the-mill motorcycle rally. I attended the 1982 British Treffen at Beaulieu and found it an easy-going mixture of Wing riders from all over Europe, including six from the USA and two from Canada.

But all the European treffen, well executed and enormous fun though they be, pale into insignificance compared with the grand daddy of all Wing gatherings, the annual Wing Ding in the United States. In 1982 and 1983 it's been held at Steamboat Springs, Colorado, and before that in Phoenix, Arizona. The event is organized by the GWRRA which likes to vary the venue to introduce members to different parts of the USA. But the association keeps the event in the same place for two to three years to ensure that local businesses give them the best possible terms. They're certainly a pretty shrewd bunch at GWRRA . . . .

After the rainstorm: riders line up for a banquet of steak, salad, baked potatoes, dessert and coffee in what must be one of the best organised camp kitchens in motorcycle rallying

Wing Ding is something else. It's a five-day celebration of the existence of the Gold Wing, a concentrated dose of flat-four bonhomie the like of which you are unlikely to experience anywhere else. Imagine Steamboat Springs, a picturesque upmarket ski resort, in mid-summer, its chalets, lodges, condominiums, apartment blocks, motels and campsites overflowing with upwards of 4000 middle-aged Gold Wingers; imagine their wives and girlfriends browsing among the fashionable boutiques that are part and parcel of any ski resort, their club colours and chapter jackets and uniforms by no means incongruous in the setting; imagine the main street of a small, well-kept American town as a sea of Gold Wings, cruising between events, exhibitions, campsites, club runs and motels—a tapestry of glittering technicolour by day and of glistening and sparkling coloured lights by night; outside every bar, coffee shop, restaurant, McDonald's, ice cream parlour and jeans store the Wings are parked, tailpipes to the kerb. And even 3000 Gold Wings can barely muster more than a muted whisper between them—above everything, the predominant noise is one of people talking.

Safety looms large in GWRRA activities. The Association even has its own safety director in Boston policeman Jim Cole. Here a Wing Dinger is put through his paces under the watchful eyes of the Motorcycle Safety Foundation at one of the skills classes at Steamboat Springs

In front of the Sheraton hotel, headquarters for the whole event, a permanent but constantly changing crowd of 100 or so riders wanders. They register for the rally, collect their badges and meal tickets and poker run tickets and timetables and associated paper-work; they walk with critical eye around the 150 Wings parked in a circle in front of the hotel and on the pavements nearby. These are the more ostentatious Wings, the ones that have come to be seen and admired above all else. Everyone glances up, dutifully, as yet another arrival nudges into the confined space while a vigilant club official points him toward a safe parking space. The owner and his lady dismount, their costume bright in the sunlight. Leaving their helmets on the red-and-white tooled leather king and queen seat, they don a couple of stetsons and mosey over to be greeted by friends from the Fresno Chapter. Stetsons are everywhere: white ones, grey ones, old ones, new ones, feathered ones, his 'n' hers matching ones.

Matching is everything. In one corner, close to the exhibition suite where all the Gold Wing goodies are soon to go on display, a gaggle of 10 riders huddle, resplendent in neat blue chapter jackets with the ubiquitous cut-off sleeves. This is the first Wing Ding for the Denver Chapter, formed in April 1982 and by August already 50-strong.

His 'n' hers is the flavour of the month. Gold lamé jackets, silver jackets, matching checked shirts 'n' jeans 'n' neckerchiefs 'n' knee-high western boots. Between the kerchiefs and the stetsons come many strong mid-Western accents and a whole bunch of other accents besides. Riders from virtually every state are here. The guy who invented white jeans could give up work soon on the strength of what's walking around in front of this hotel. If he was the same guy who invented stetsons as a fashion accessory then he's probably retired already—somewhere close to Fort Knox.

Half a dozen guys are constantly polishing their Wings even though the judging for best bike is still two days away. Country-and-western songs spill forth from a dozen cassette decks to keep the polishers company. Little groups of Wing experts stand around shooting the breeze while others stoop to inspect some detail of a drastically altered GL. 'That,' says one white-haired old-timer, pointing to a grossly over-dressed machine, 'is a '78.'

'No,' says his partner, a couple of years younger and dressed in identical chapter jacket, 'it's a '79.'

'It's a '78, gotta be, 'cos they didn't start chroming them brackets till '79.'

Everywhere fingers poke, eyes peer, people smile. A constant flow of riders strolls in and out of the main doors of the Sheraton. If only one in three buys a drink to stay cool, the hotel barman is having a busy day. I wander over to the registration tent to collect my registration pack. All the documentation is neatly ordered. You get a metal lapel badge with your first name on it, two headlight stickers to show you've paid your dues, a ticket for the official banquet, a Wing Ding programme, a good-quality metal Wing Ding badge, and sundry offers from local businesses. I choose between an 'exclusive to Gold Wingers' buffet breakfast for $3.95 at The Charcoal House between Safeway and Wendy's in the Sundance Plaza; coupons for $1 off dinner at the Riverbend Inn on Highway 40 and at The Charcoal House; a free glass of wine or beer at the Old West Steakhouse; a free Steamboat patch from Inside Edge Sports; and a free ride on the hydrolube giant water slide at Hot Mineral Springs.

The public relations effort by the GWRRA in advance of Wing Ding has paid off. The boutiques had signs out front welcoming Wing Dingers. A big page three feature in the local *Steamboat Whistle* placed by GWRRA national director Paul Hildebrand predicted that the riders would spend between $1 million and $2 million in Steamboat during the course of Wing Ding, and that may have had something to do with the warmth of the welcome. As I wander in and out of the boutiques looking for the odd souvenir, or Levi's at prices that would make any European weep with envy, one or two shopkeepers tell me that the prediction has fallen a bit flat. 'They may be spending a million bucks,' says the girl in The Homesteader, 'but they sure ain't spending it here!' She concedes, though, that a shop which specialises in pine kitchen accessories, brass lamps and the like is unlikely to make a killing at a motorcycle event—even a Gold Wing event. . . .

The Wing Ding programme of activities is well organized. First off is the crowning of the Wing Ding Queen at the Sheraton poolside at noon on the Friday of Labour Day weekend. I guess the title must have fallen on one of the younger ladies, but I missed the chance to find out because I was half a day's ride away at the time in Arches National Park, Utah. Pretty girls you can see everywhere but I'd travelled 8000 miles and wasn't going to miss Arches for *anything*.

The exhibition of accessories, touring equipment, trailers and bikes opens for a few hours each day. I'll catch that later. Meantime, the Motorcycle Safety Foundation is running skills classes outside, the chapters battle it out in slow-motion and water-carrying races, and the 'most uniform' contests get underway. Those uniforms would get laughed off many a motorcycle rally site in Britain or Europe, but that probably says more about the immaturity of some European riders than it does about the Americans' passion for dressing up. It's all part of the GWRRA's valiant and successful effort to smarten up motorcycling's public image.

The world's only Wing-mounted motorcycle display team? Members of the Gold Wing Owners Club of Great Britain give one of their first public displays of low-speed formation riding in the grounds of Beaulieu, the stately home venue for the 1982 British Treffen

Honda Gold Wing

Opposite page **Palm trees at sunset at a roadside diner in Indio, in the Mojave Desert. It's eight o'clock and the temperature is still over 100 degrees F. Behind the fairing it's hotter than hell**

Below **With days still to go before the motorcycle judging at Wing Ding, riders everywhere were polishing every last inch of their show bikes. Two days later it rained, and they had to start all over . . .**

Saturday offers the same or very similar options and heralds the start of a series of seminars in which Honda technical staff give lectures and answer questions on various aspects of owning, riding and maintaining a Gold Wing. Saturday is also distinguished by an impressive open-air banquet held in one of the large ski-area car parks. Tables and chairs for the multitude are laid out with cutlery under a vast, open-sided marquee while six long lines of Wing Dingers queue for barbecued steaks, jacket potatoes, salad, starters and dessert at three field kitchens. As we wait in line, waitresses serve drinks to order at extra charge.

As I reach the all-important steak-serving point the weather, which has changed from a week of blistering sunshine to overcast overnight, breaks. Huge raindrops spatter briefly and some of the cognoscenti behind me run for cover. Within seconds we are in the middle of a torrential downpour. But the chefs serve steaks, potatoes and all the trimmings with complete calm to those of us hungry enough to stay put. Then, as we run with plates piled high for the shelter of the marquee the staff are already putting plastic sheets over the field kitchens, the coffee stands and the bar. Within 30 seconds everything is more or less watertight as the rain doubles its intensity and the wind threatens to blow the marquee all the way to Missouri. It's all over in five minutes and the staff begin their preparations for the second sitting. The food is good and the atmosphere friendly. They run out of coffee just as it gets to my turn but what the heck. As they clear the tables for the next 2000 hungry souls I'm lost in conversation with a big Texan who bemoans the fact that he has ridden all the way from Texas for Wing Ding. It was better, he maintains, when it was held in Phoenix. How had he travelled to Steamboat Springs? Through Utah, is the reply. 'Ain't nuthin' worth a goddam in Utah except goddam desert,' he

RUBBER KNEE GRIP

Colour 2,3,4,5—
Opposite page The bike
that started it all (*top*)—
the 1975 GL1000 Gold
Wing was the second
quickest production
motorcycle of its day. It
could have looked very
different, as this factory
sketch (*bottom*) reveals. If
Honda had not developed
the CBX, perhaps this
sports version of the Wing
would have gone into
production. *This page* Two
American Wing Nuts quiz
Gold Wing designer Shuji
Tanaka about aspects of
the Aspencade at an
owners' club gathering.
Rider feedback played a
large part in the design of
the Aspencade. This
beautifully customised
Interstate (*below*) was
spotted at the 1982 British
Treffen

Colour 7—
This vision in burgundy,
chrome and hand-tooled
leather would stand out
from the crowd most days
of the week; at Wing
Ding, however, it was just
one of many

Colour 6—
Imaginative murals adorn
the fairings, tanks and
luggage of many
customised Wings. This
lady (*left*), on an
impeccable French GL at
a British Treffen, is
typical of the best

Colour 8—
Left A mobile tribute to the chrome-plater's art. Wings like this one keep an ever-growing, evermore-inventive bolt-on accessory industry in business. The attention to detail must be seen to be believed

Colour 10—
The author's Aspencade at the entrance to Zion National Park, Utah, as he took the scenic route from Los Angeles to Wing Ding at Steamboat Springs. Even on 600-mile days, his only complaint was engine heat thrown up by the fairing

Colour 9—
Below Allen Cutler's rainbow rig set him back about $13,000. He designed the paint job with his children and girlfriend Phyllis by working with paints on a black-and-white blow-up of the motorcycle and trailer. Zak, his German Shepherd, takes in the scenery from his trailer seat without complaint.

Wherever they stop, as here at Bryce Canyon, Utah, cameras appear as if from nowhere . . .

confides. Had he not seen any of the spectacular national parks such as Bryce Canyon, Zion or Capital Reef that make Utah such a gem for the touring rider? 'Can't say I have,' he replies.

Outside it's growing dark as I head back into town with Allan Cutler and girlfriend Phyllis on their unique 'Zak's Pak' Wing. The main street is busy with brightly lit Wings purring its length. Back at the Cutler campsite I run across a guy whose Wing is lit up like the proverbial Christmas tree. The flexible strip lights so beloved of Wing owners in the US adorn every conceivable inch of his machine and its trailer. He even has a string of little lights around the circumference of each front disc brake shield! We leave him pondering how to fit an extra strip of lights to his saddlebags and ride back to town to watch the endless parade of mobile tributes to the customisers' catalogues.

An air-conditioned ice cream parlour offers a temporary respite from the heat. We relive the good old days of hell-raising with an elderly Harley rider who'd come to town to see what all the fuss was about. He reckons that motorcycling has changed since his heyday but admits that the change has been for the better. He even likes Gold Wings. . . . Back at the ski area the bars and restaurants are doing a roaring trade. We end the day in a large jacuzzi in the ground floor of a luxurious condo with a middle-aged rider who couldn't afford the time to ride to Wing Ding from California and so had flown to Steamboat in his own aircraft! Another Wing Dinger gives a blow-by-blow account of how he bought his first K2—'I fell in love with the blue paint job'—and explains how the purchase was a joint decision by him and his wife. A lot of wives play quite a major role in the purchase of a Wing, it seems, but I guess that's true of any large touring bike. 'If you're gonna blow $8000 on a motorcycle and I'm

Opposite page **The 1983 Aspencade featured Honda's latest liquid-crystal wizardry, with digital readouts for speedometer, tachometer, gear position and tripmeter, a linear graph for the tachometer and bar charts for suspension pressure, fuel level and engine temperature**

What happens to motorcyclists when they turn 40? In the United States, at least, a fair number of 'em buy Gold Wings. Wing Ding attracts a smattering of owners in their 20s, but the average age is older than you'd expect

gonna have to sit on the thing for our vacation then I'd better be sure I like it' appears to be the rationale. My wife operates the same way. Makes a lot of sense.

Sunday dawns wet and it promises to get a lot wetter. The poker run is scheduled for this morning and I ride down to the starting point in my rainsuit, wondering whether the event will be cancelled or postponed. After all, European riders *know* that Americans don't ride in the rain if they can possibly avoid it. And surely none of these guys, who've been polishing their Wings for days now, are going to risk getting them wet and dirty for the sake of a poker run?

The assembly area is overflowing with riders. They line up six abreast at the registration table, old and young alike. Bikes are everywhere. GWRRA officials marshall the riders into small groups and send them on their way. And these aren't just the plainer, more standard Wings: the show bikes, the custom dressers, the exotic paint jobs and the mobile monuments to the chrome-platers' art are there too. GWRRA director Paul Hildebrand is among them. Nobody's going to let a little rainfall stop them from having some fun when there's some riding to be done. . . . Visiting Irish author, born and bred in the land of eternal rain, forgets everything he has ever heard about Americans and wet-weather motorcycling.

Even Allan and Phyllis are there with the ultra-exotic $13,000 trailer rig, Zak's Pak. Allan has never ridden in rain before (so some of the stories are true!) and his immaculate outfit is entered in the bike judging tomorrow, but he's planning to ride up to his brother's mountain cabin at Grand Lake—about two hours away at about 9000 feet in the Rockies. That sounds even more fun than a poker run, so we head off together.

The steady rain becomes a downpour as we splash past hordes of Wing Dingers returning from one of the first poker run stops. The way everybody waves at us it is obvious they are enjoying themselves despite the weather. It's an incredible sight, these oh-so-lovingly prepared dressers out there on the road getting wet, dirty and grimy! The temperature drops to 43 degrees F, the downpour continues and the mist obscures what Allan's brother Ed assures me is a spectacular view of the Rockies around Denver. After days of riding in 100-degree temperatures across sun-scorched deserts I now feel right at home. This could so easily be North Wales.

Back in Steamboat, the rain has dried up, the sun is back and it's time for the pocket-racer heats. These are miniature motorcycles that look tiny under a four-year-old, let alone a full-grown Wing-sized adult. But men, women and children all line up in their respective heats to try their skill at this unique form of racing.

Time for a last look at the exhibition in a large suite at the Sheraton. On display for the first time are the 1983 Wings. The improvements over the '82s get widespread approval. The removable rear mudguard section strikes a note of accord with anyone who's had a rear-wheel flat on a Wing. The box-section swingarm and the V4-style front fork brace seem a great idea. Riders agree that the 11-spoke cast alloy wheels look really neat and Aspencade afficionados nod appreciatively as they note the higher placement of the radio channel-seeking thumb-switch which previously was too close to the dipswitch. The gradual improvements and refinements continue.

Elsewhere in the show the accessory manufacturers are having a field day. Chromed disc and caliper covers and radiator covers are going well on the Big Bike Parts stand. The Cycle-Lite brake light is attracting some interest from the ever-safety-conscious Wing Dingers. Ther's a perpetual huddle around the CC Products stand as riders examine a neat fork brace and reinforcement for Gold Wing swingarms. There's a neat supercharged Wing on the stand too, attracting a lot of comment and questions. The multi-coloured stitched leather king and queen Utopia seats by The Seat Shop are another focal point. And the major accessory suppliers such as Drag Specialities, Custom Dressers and Motorcycle Products Unlimited are doing a roaring trade in items such as chrome ride-off stands, case savers, floorboards, backrests, pipe extensions and sheepskin seat covers. There's a trend toward functional accessories from the traditional suppliers of bolt-on chrome goodies. Custom Dressers, for instance, are getting into fork springs, rear shocks and turbo kits. Other stands offer electronic cruise control, radar detection devices and, from Kerker, a centre stand device that the rider can operate from the saddle for $189. And of course the trailer manufacturers are there in force: Road Runner, Poli-Tron, Motavation, Travlite and Smitty's. Stereos, clothing, luggage and the complete range of Hondaline accessories are also on offer.

Meanwhile the seminar programme continues. You can learn all about spark plugs, suspension, trailers, sidecars, on-bike entertainment systems, and insurance, or attend two Honda technical clinics. In the basement of one of the car parks you can have your Wing serviced by mechanics from Sunnyslope Honda of Phoenix with all their mobile workshop equipment, or have one of several pinstripe artists customise your machine while you wait. The bars and

Wing Dingers line up to sign on for the Poker Run. Within the hour, they're all out in the Rockies getting cold and wet while their glittering machinery gets dirty and grimy. The 'dresser' image is only part of the game – these guys are into *riding* . . .

restaurants spill over with riders and the subdued procession of Wings to and from the many Wing Ding centres continues late into the evening.

Monday brings the eagerly awaited bike judging, with some worthy winners and as always some unlucky losers. As far as I can tell, Zak's Pak isn't in the awards this time. In Britain or in Europe this rig would have walked off with all the show awards but I guess the competition was pretty intense. Again you can choose between the seminars, yet more Battles of the Chapters, the men's pocket racers grand prix and the exhibition before the awards presentation in the evening and dancing to local band Cow Patty and the Meadow Muffins. Those with any time or energy left spend Tuesday shooting the rapids on the Colorado River Adventure organised by the GWRRA or merely availing themselves of the local swimming, golfing or horse-riding facilities. Then the world's best organised motorcycle social event is over for another year.

That's not to say Wing Ding is everyone's cup of tea. There was some dissent in the ranks. Several riders reckoned the GWRRA should lay on more events. 'You ride 3000 miles for what?' one rider said. 'There should be evening seminars or shows or something. This event is open 9–9.30, that one 2–4 pm. What do you do after that?' Other riders felt that the $35 entry fee was too high, especially since it costs $45 if you don't pre-register. 'That's 90 bucks for a couple,' another rider told me. 'You just don't get enough for that sort of money.'

They may have a point. Some riders saved themselves $90 by attending the event but not registering, thereby missing the exhibits, the banquet and the poker run, but nonetheless still being able to soak up the atmosphere, meet other Wing Nuts, look at the more exotic dressers and generally have a good time. But the fact that most of the 4000-odd who came and paid didn't complain suggests that the fee is realistic and doesn't overtax the resources of people who can tie up so much money in their bikes in the first place.

Having been to Wing Ding, I reckon that every Wing owner who gets the chance ought to attend the event—even if only once. It's the world's greatest collection of Gold Wings and their enthusiastic owners and you'll feel right at home there.

5 The flourishing aftermarket

If you bought a Gold Wing back in 1975 and wanted to use it for anything like its intended purpose, you had to look around for such basic necessities as a luggage rack, saddlebags and a fairing. The large established luggage and touring equipment suppliers were not slow to meet the demand by adapting existing products with purpose-designed brackets to match the Wing's mounting holes. But in 1975 that was about the extent of the aftermarket range for the 1000 cc newcomer. Try to search for even the most basic bolt-on item for a Wing today and you stumble into cornucopia of specially produced accoutrements listed in catalogues as thick as motorcycle magazines. The Gold Wing aftermarket business today turns over an estimated $50 million and the

The GL1000 had barely hit the streets before established accessory companies like Daytona and Lester were offering their fairings and cast alloy wheels to fit the newcomer. A whole new multi-million dollar industry was being born

range and type of equipment available is growing almost daily. 'Personalising' your Gold Wing has become big, big business.

In the beginning, the majority of add-on items were strictly functional. One of the first things most American owners with any sensitivity for their backsides did was to chuck the stock dualseat in favour of something a little less flat and a little more plush. The original dualseat was flat, hard and uncomfortable. More than 32 per cent of the 582 Wing Nuts who took part in a *Road Rider* magazine survey in 1976 rated the saddle as the bike's worst feature. One reader, Judy Craft from Ovid, New York, wrote: 'Japanese seat no fit American backside.' It didn't do a lot for the European or Australian backside either, but the Americans were the first to get to the bottom of the problem with custom-designed, two-tier king-and-queen seats that relieved long-distance numbness. They soon became a standard feature of almost all customized Wings. Honda themselves took note of the criticism but it wasn't until 1977 that a new seat appeared from the factory. Even then, although it was an improvement, it still left plenty of scope for the aftermarket suppliers to do even better. The stock seat was improved again in 1978, and again in 1980, and again in 1981 . . . but the custom seats still keep right on selling. Today, the stock seat rates as one of the best in all of motorcycling, but there will always be a market for something a little more individual.

Next item on the agenda for change by those first Wing owners was the handlebars. Many riders considered them too far forward. Some switched to alternative bars, but that was a troublesome operation since the early models had the wiring to the handlebar switches routed through the bars themselves,

Not all the bolt-ons are cosmetic. This CC Products demonstrator is fitted with the company's supercharger, fork brace, swingarm reinforcement and Motocross Fox gas shocks

while others installed 'setbacks' to mount the bars several inches nearer the rider. Then some entrepreneur had the bright idea of selling setback brackets with the Gold Wing insignia mounted on top, and the fledgling Gold Wing aftermarket was up and running.

While the custom chrome companies were dreaming up all sorts of gadgets and gizmos to prise money out of the hands of Wing owners, the owners themselves were far more interested in improving ride comfort. Suspension compliance was not the GL1000's strong suit. The front fork springs were designed to be stiff to prevent the wide four-cylinder motor grounding in corners. Ironically, the fork legs themselves were not quite stiff *enough* and were prone to flexing fore and aft under heavy braking with the machine fully loaded. But what worried most riders was the harsh ride they gave. The rear shock absorbers allowed the rear end to wallow in corners, did nothing for ride comfort, bottomed-out too easily and were generally considered useless after only 4000 miles. A high degree of static friction didn't help matters by ensuring that the forks hardly responded at all to minor road irregularities such as concrete expansion joints.

The rear-end problem was the easiest to solve and the stock shocks invariably were junked in favour of Konis (the most popular alternative of the day), Girlings, S&W variable shocks, S&W air adjustables, and Boge Mulholland rebuildables. The Gold Wing probably did more for the fortunes of shock absorber manufacturers than any other modern motorcycle—although several others sure tried hard! Why those shock manufacturers never tried—or, if they did try, never succeeded—to break into the Honda camp as

Nestling between the top tubes is the CC Products supercharger. The two upper engine mounting lugs have been relocated and one frame cross-member removed to accommodate it. The $2500 conversion gives an 11.7-second standing quarter mile at 5–6 lb of boost

original equipment suppliers based on their demonstrable superiority never ceases to amaze me. Perhaps it had more to do with politics, nationalism and existing Honda contracts than with choosing the best system. In any event, the replacement shocks gave an immediate and worthwhile improvement, just as they had done in years past for the CB750 Four.

Up front, owners experimented with different weights of oil in the fork legs. Some found a partial cure with automatic transmission fluid and/or S&W fork springs, but the problem was not satisfactorily solved by Honda until the introduction of air suspension as standard on the GL1100 in 1980.

Another problem causing concern to early Wing owners was tyre wear. Some owners were getting only 4000 to 5000 miles out of the original rear Bridgestone and at around $50 a time this was proving kind of expensive for high-mileage riders. Some riders were getting almost twice that tyre mileage, so some of the blame may have rested with riding at continuous high speeds with slightly under-inflated tyres at more than the rated gross vehicle weight. In any event, competition hotted up between Dunlop, Goodyear and Bridgestone to develop a tyre that would last longer.

Possibly the ugliest addition to any Gold Wing is the liquefied petroleum gas (LPG) conversion used by some riders in Europe. The system runs cleaner than the normal set-up, offers slightly less power, but adds 300 miles to the Wing's touring range

Wet-weather braking was another area where the original Gold Wing left plenty of room for improvement. The operational time lag in the rain was quite unacceptable and indeed the Wing was the subject of a US Department of Transportation recall on this account. In Britain, a company called Trimat Engineering was being run by Wing owner (and currently chairman of the Gold Wing Owners Club of Great Britain) Mike Bridge. At that time there was a general perception that the fault lay with the stainless steel disc material. Italian bikes such as Laverda, Moto Guzzi and Ducati had much better wet-weather braking performance and were fitted instead with cast iron discs. So Mike turned out some cast iron discs for his Wing, fitted them and found an improvement. He then put the conversion on the market in the UK, not just for Wings but for a variety of other popular Japanese machines. I tried a set on my Yamaha XS750 at the time and felt they made matters worse, if anything, and so switched back again. Mike still rides with those cast iron discs to this day and continues to find them excellent. In the meantime the researchers at Britain's Transport and Road Research Laboratory (TRRL) had determined that the critical factor was not disc material but pad material. Sintered pads soon became all the rage and appeared as original equipment on many Japanese bikes—including the Wing.

Owners of 1975, '76 and '77 Wings often complained that the overall gearing of the machine was too high. They found the bike lugging at legal speeds, requiring downshifting for overtaking and hill-climbing, and found these problems exacerbated when hitched to a sidecar or trailer. So a company called GEM Products in Illinois came up with an ingenious device to alleviate these characteristics: a ring and pinion set for the rear hub which reduced the standard final drive ratio of 3.4:1 to a lower 4.0:1. The conversion cost about $170 in parts and took about two hours to complete. Results were good. On the open road, the GEM unit caused the Wing to run at about 750 to 1000 rpm higher than standard at cruising speeds. The penalty for this was a five per cent rise in fuel consumption, but the benefits included greatly improved overtaking ability, even with a trailer attached, easier hill-climbing and significantly reduced drivetrain snatch in city traffic. Honda then solved the

'Japanese seat no fit American backside', said one GL owner in a *Road Rider* survey. Thousands of fellow riders thought likewise, and a replacement seat was one of the most popular accessories until Honda learned the lesson and offered a better seat on the GL1100

problem its own way in 1978 by redesigning the engine to give a flatter power band over a much wider range than before.

By 1976, however, the Gold Wing accessory industry was taking off in a big way. Engine protector bars, floorboards, fairings, saddlebags, racks, backrests, topboxes, chromed disc brake covers, Electra Glide lookalike front fenders, disc caliper covers, silencer extension tips and even a Gold Wing tank-top CB radio all hit the streets in an inordinately short space of time in the USA. In Europe, and particularly in Britain, things were a little leaner on the accessory front.

Gradually the list of accessories tailor-made specifically for the GL series blossomed to include everything from gold-plated radiator grilles to handlebar-mounted drink holders. The cult of Wing dressing became an art and a major hobby in itself.

There are now more than 30 companies worldwide producing aftermarket accessories specifically for the Gold Wing. Those are the companies I have been able to trace and the number excludes the fairing and luggage equipment suppliers that include the Wing in a long list of models catered for. There undoubtedly are other, more obscure outfits in the Gold Wing accessory trade as well.

Perhaps the best known is Custom Dressers, both because of their product range and the fact that they advertise heavily in the motorcycle touring press. They actually produce *two* catalogues of goodies for Wings—one for the Interstate and Aspencade models, and another for all the other Wings! If you see a dressed Wing on the highway anywhere in the US and increasingly also in Europe, the chances are that at least some—and in many cases all—of the

If you're touring you need saddlebags, so you might as well have saddlebag protection bars. If you've got saddlebag protection bars, why not add lights. And why not have a new taillight, and . . .

glittering bits come from Custom Dressers.

Their product lists are endless but include exhaust extensions, fairings, vented chromed transmission covers, carb and plug covers, handlebar clamp covers, floor boards, gold-plated Gold Wing emblems in all shapes and sizes, chrome saddlebag protectors, lighted chrome front fender protectors, unlighted version of same, front brake caliper covers, chrome fairing shields, extra-tall windscreens, vinyl chrome windscreen edging, chrome front brake reservoir covers, chrome radiator grilles, engine spoilers, chrome venturi for fairing lowers, driving light mounts, driving lights, backrests and armrests, saddlebag lid guards, chrome engine guards, front fenders, saddlebag rock guards, bolt head covers, chrome saddlebag rails, inlaid fairing tonneau covers, headlamp visors, custom seats, custom paint jobs, 'mini' fairing lowers, heel-and-toe gearshift pedals, 16-inch wheels, foot pegs, sidestand extender, dummy tank covers, disc brake covers, top box and saddlebag bumper bars with inbuilt strip lights, and a whole bunch more besides.

Drag Specialties is another major supplier of Wing bolt-ons, offering similar items to Custom Dressers plus a number of extras such as chrome swingarm plug covers, tank-top and topbox luggage racks, lower fork leg light brackets, ride-off centrestands, fuel pump covers, lighted license plate bars, chrome rocker covers, chrome timing belt covers, fairing vent grilles, belt buckles, saddlebags, tour boxes, chrome fork leg caps, and even a specially formulated Wing Wax to keep everything looking smart!

Variations on the same theme come from Touring Specialties of Arlington, Texas; Can Am Marketing of Mentor, Ohio; D&D Enterprises of Palmdale, California; Gene's Gallery of Springfield, Missouri; Accessory House of Long

Accessories Unlimited is the name of this company, and the name speaks for itself. You name it, they have it. The sea of chrome-plate continues around the Wing Ding exhibition hall, reflecting the names of a dozen other suppliers

Beach, California; Phoenix Touring Specialties of where you'd expect; Accessories Unlimited of Saugus, California; Markland Industries of Santa Ana, California; Motorcycle Products Unlimited; and certainly not last and by no means least, Hondaline in the US and Hondastyle in the UK. All of these bolt-ons are available by mail from the manufacturers or through a network of distributors and motorcycle dealers throughout the US and, to a lesser degree, parts of Europe and Australia.

In recent years there has been a trend toward more functional accessories as riders have tried to improve on the basic factory package. Fuel capacity at 4.2 Imperial gallons (5.3 US gallons) has never been anything to write home about on a machine with a touring range of only 160–175 miles (if you get a range of 200 miles out of your Wing you ride more sedately than I do). One solution has been pannier fuel tanks that attach in place of the plastic sidepanels. Popular in Continental Europe, they hold one Imperial gallon each and stretch the touring range to a more realistic 250 miles. The main drawback is that they're plain ugly. Uglier still is the liquefied petroleum gas (LPG) conversion being used by some European riders. This puts an eight-gallon LPG tank on the rear carrier, adding about 300 miles to the petrol range. A simple switch allows the rider to convert from one energy source to the other. There's no excuse for running out of fuel with this system, but the weight of an eight-gallon tank on the rack makes the conversion more suitable for sidecar than solo use. Riders with the LPG system report that it runs cleaner than petrol but offers a little less power.

Another interesting aftermarket item on the fuel supply side is the Spider intake system from HP Products of Santa Cruz, California. This is a twin-choke Weber carburettor which replaces the standard four Keihins. The manufacturers claim better throttle response, more low-end and mid-range torque, a smoother power band, a major reduction in off-idle hesitation, and

The flourishing aftermarket

Opposite page **The rear end gets as much attention as the front, with a multitude of wrap-around bars, dozens of accessory lights, chromed tow bars, taillight grilles, extra stop lamps . . .**

Chrome covers the throttle linkages, the spark plug leads and the rocker boxes. This bike has floor boards, highway pegs and a ride-off centre-stand

better fuel mileage at cruising speeds. Some people may think it worth the $350 asking price just because it eliminates the four-carb synchronisation task. HP Products also offers a dipstick which bolts in place of the standard oil drain plug and incorporates its own drain plug. The dipstick is popular with Wing sidecar owners because the chair obscures the oil-level sight window.

Innovation on the fuel intake front comes from CC Products of Los Gatos, California, which offers a supercharger for the Wing at around $2500 all-in. Their aim was also to eliminate the need for multi-carb synchronisation and to overcome the lack of mid-range torque, hard starting and general cold-bloodedness. They looked to supercharging because turbochargers, they felt, would always suffer from unacceptable time lag and involve complex mechanical and electronic solutions. The CC supercharger is belt-driven from the same shaft which drives the cam belts. CC reckons that the Wing engine is virtually bulletproof and so far they report the supercharger to be as trouble-free as the stock aspiration system. They claim easy starting, smooth idling, same fuel consumption as standard if the rider resists the temptation to perform burnouts everywhere, an ability to run on regular fuel without detonation—and instant and rapid acceleration at a touch of the throttle in fourth or even fifth gears. They claim a standing quarter mile time of 11.7 seconds and a terminal speed in the quarter of 112–118 mph from a 1982 GL1100 ridden at sea level with the supercharger being driven at 10 per cent under crank speed and with 5 to 6 lb of boost. That sort of muscle could embarrass more than a few CBX and XS1100 riders! The only modifications necessary for the installation are the relocation of the two upper engine mounting lugs and the narrowing or removal of the frame cross-member in front of the fuel tank. Even the exhaust system remains as stock—it gives the

This guy's got one of the most impressive seats around, the Honda radio, cassette deck and CB, a neat luggage grid on the tank, and about as much chrome-plate as space will allow. Even the centre-stand is plated

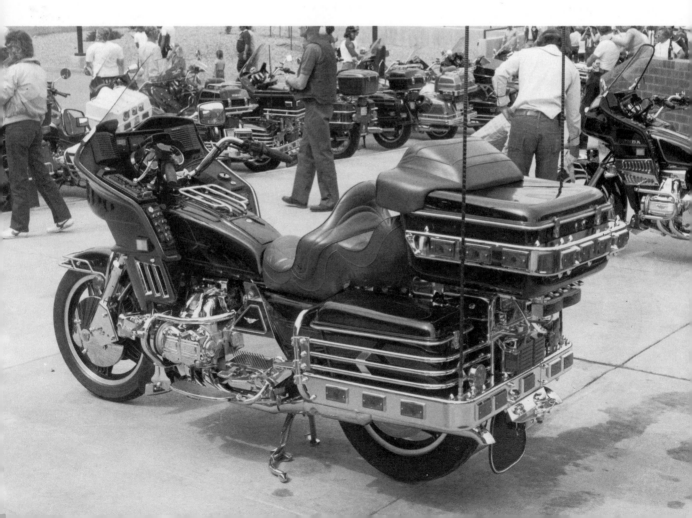

best performance, says CC.

Exhaust systems is one area where most Wing owners appear happy to stick with the factory's choice. The quietness of the Wing is one of its best features as a touring bike, one of its most endearing features as a socially acceptable front-runner for motorcycling, and one of the things the critics deride. In fact, the early models were so hushed that Honda introduced a slightly more throaty—but still very subdued—system in 1978 in response to owner feedback. The original '75–'77 system was a black, car-like affair which was heavy, rusted all too easily and to many people looked ugly. The '78s were not only throatier but the black system was replaced by a more attractive all-chrome set-up that must have had wider appeal.

It was the rotting of the original system and its high replacement cost that caused many owners to look to replacement systems from Jardine, Kerker, Winning, Campbell Geometrics in the UK, DG Exhausts and Yoshimura. A company called Breakwell and Green at Long Eaton in England sells a neat stainless steel replacement system for around £250 that should eliminate the problem of rust permanently. Invariably the chromed replacement systems look better, last longer and sound sportier, but none really come up to the level of hush provided by the stock item.

The ignition system was another candidate for replacement by owners of early models. The stock contact breaker system was blamed by many for misfiring under load, poor points and condenser life, spark plug fouling, premature spark plug failure and awkwardness in setting the ignition timing. Consequently, the makers of aftermarket electronic ignition systems did good business out of Gold Wings until Honda introduced its own electronic system with the 1980 GL1100. GL1000 owner Ron Rennie from Los Angeles has had

Next pages **Fred and Tina Wagner achieved a far more tasteful effect (*left*) with less chrome and rather fewer lights. Hand-tooled seat and backrest are nice touches. Not everyone opts for the Honda sound equipment. This Wing Dinger (*right*) has gone instead for Cycle Sound radio-cassette and a Beltex CB transceiver**

Below **There are limits to good taste, and a lot of folk would argue that this Wing from New Jersey has gone over the top. The rider would be lucky to escape with his dignity from a Laverda or Ducati owners' meeting!**

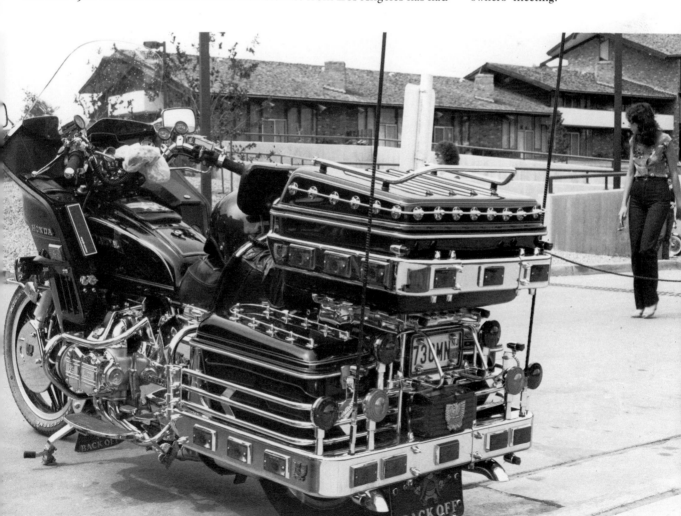

no problems since he changed to a Prestolite system five years ago. He now changes his plugs once a year. Mike Bridge is one of many British Wing Nuts who found salvation in the Piranha electronic ignition system. Another UK favourite is the Boyer Bransden, while other systems are available from Jardine (the Ignitor), Lucas and other suppliers.

Two final functional aftermarket items of note both come from CC Products: a front fork brace and a reinforced swingarm. Together they are claimed to provide a significant increase in chassis stiffness and a consequent improvement in handling. The fork brace comes with or without optional fender trim in gloss black or chrome and is designed to reduce fork flex and steering wobble by tying the sliders together at the fork's weak mid-point. The

An awful lot of riders couldn't live with the stock shocks. In Europe, they changed to Koni or Girling units until S&Ws became widely available. In the US, S&Ws were the popular alternative. These Motocross Fox dual-spring gas shocks with remote reservoir are used on the CC Products supercharged Wing. Cost: $325!

swingarm reinforcement is a light triangulated section of tubular steel which is TIG-welded to the underside of the stock swingarm to reduce flex and better resist the deforming effects of heavy loads.

The bulk of the aftermarket industry feeding the Gold Wing population, however, survives not on functional items but on chrome embellishments. Most of these pieces of brightwork are conceived in the adopted homeland of the Gold Wing, the United States, but are made in the Far East. The majority of the items on sale in Europe are imported from the US, often at extortionate prices that have varied surprisingly from country to country. A radiator grille can cost half as much in Belgium as is charged for an identical grille in Britain, for instance. Many British Wing Nuts have found it cheaper to ride to the Continent on holiday, kit the bike out with the desired bolt-ons, and ride home again—all for less than the cost of buying the bits in Britain. An unhappy feature of the British accessory market has always been that, whatever the current exchange rate, American accessories invariably cost in sterling in the UK the same figure as they cost in dollars in the US. That's life. It also helps to account for the relative paucity of full-dress Wings in Britain compared to, say, Germany. The rest of the reason is one of national tastes. To an American brought up on the overly stylised cars of the 1950s and '60s, and familiar with the excesses of the Electra Glide customising set, a Wing dresser is as natural and American as grits, the flag and apple pie. To a British rider, brought up in a less garish atmosphere and taught to appreciate the handling virtues of Triumphs and Nortons, the stock Gold Wing at 650 lb is pushing things a bit. Adding maybe 250 lb of extras is seen as a kind of madness in Britain—even by a good number of Wing enthusiasts. Yet Larry Tietz of Honda R&D tells of one American Wing Nut who has a 1100-lb 1979 Gold Wing. 'He says it handles real good,' says Larry. 'He's proud of it.' Each, as they say, to his own. . . .

Perhaps the most surprising thing about the Gold Wing accessory business is that Honda in Japan waited so long to cash in on the aftermarket bonanza by supplying as standard all the things most Wing buyers were adding on themselves. The extra profit potential was enormous. But it took a full five years before Honda unveiled what many riders believe was the touring machine they should have made in the first place: the Gold Wing Interstate, or Gold Wing De Luxe as the marketing men dubbed it in parts of Europe for some obscure reason.

King-and-queen seats? The Interstate had one. Electronic ignition? That too. Air suspension front and rear? Yep. Full touring fairing? The Interstate's is the best in the business. Saddlebags and top case? Yes, and these were colour-matched to the bike. Quartz clock? Of course. AM/FM stereo and intercom? You'll find few better in any accessory catalogue. In short, the Interstate more closely reflected what the market researchers found Wing buyers wanted. It gave them the complete package more cheaply and arguably to a higher quality standard than they could have obtained for themselves from disparate sources. The Gold Wing had found a new maturity. And the accessory manufacturers? Their response was to churn out a whole new gaggle of goodies for the Interstate and to rely on a goodly proportion of Wing buyers being contrary enough not to like Honda's version of the complete touring bike and instead to dress for themselves the unadorned basic model. And even with the introduction in 1982 of the still-jazzier Aspencade, the accessory suppliers have yet to be proved wrong on either count.

6 The sidecar brigade

This 1975 GL1000 (*below*) needed no modification to take this single-seat sports chair, shown at the 1976 Paris Motorcycle Show. At the other end of the spectrum is this Interstate with Equalean sidecar, futuristic in concept and design (*right*). More radical changes for this British Interstate (*below right*) with EML Earles-type forks, smaller diameter alloy wheels and car tyres

If the Gold Wing's specification made it the world's best touring motorcycle in solo use, then the same specification made it also the world's most suitable sidecar machine. The engine has ample power and torque for the task, the shaft drive is better suited to the extra loads than any chain, and the frame is strong enough to accept the increased stresses without modification. Small wonder, then, that so many sidecars have found their way to the flank of a Wing.

Sidecars have enjoyed a strong revival in the past six years after a long period in the doldrums. Most major sidecar manufacturers offer fittings to suit the Gold Wing, and installation can be completed in a weekend by a moderately competent owner. Most fittings provide for attachment to the motorcycle frame at four points: just beneath the dummy fuel tank, at the base of the engine in front, at the base of the sidepanel and on the frame tube under the seat.

The type of fittings vary from one manufacturer to another, but those supplied by Watsonian are fairly typical: a large bolt spanning the two frame

Honda Gold Wing

This neat little outfit (*below*) at Steamboat Springs is called *Beer Boy* and the trailer is decorated with the Coors logo. Like many Wing outfits, the motorcycle is virtually stock mechanically. Another Equalean sidecar (*right*), and the owner on the left is busy explaining how the sidecar leans with the bike into curves. And (*below right*) another view of Beer Boy, one of the best-presented Wing-powered sidecar outfits around

downtubes at the top front mount, carrying a swan-neck fitting; a conventional clamp at front bottom; a plate spanning the converging downtubes below the sidepanel at bottom back; and another conventional bolt clamped to the frame tube at top back.

First-time Wing sidecar fitters need two days to complete the job: one day for initial fitting, the second for lining everything up. Most Wing-based sidecar outfits are set up with between $\frac{1}{2}$-inch and 1-inch toe-in and very little sidecar lean-out. Fitting and correctly setting-up a sidecar is an art. Most sidecar makers will do the job for a fee, but the Clymer Gold Wing workshop manual has a section on fitting sidecars which comes highly recommended by the *cognoscenti*. Squire, a leading British sidecar builder, even offers a universal clamp which bolts to the handlebar and a fixed point like a garage door to make the operation easier, since you can't set-up an outfit with the bike on its centre stand.

The standard Gold Wing front forks are adequate for the job of steering the outfit, but a steering damper is essential to eliminate judder. Most riders keep it screwed down hard. But keeping the standard fork set-up means that the steering geometry is not ideal for a sidecar outfit and the steering consequently is a little on the heavy side. The cheapest solution is to fit wider, higher handlebars to give more leverage.

Increasingly, owners of Wing-based sidecar outfits are fitting aftermarket leading-link forks with their shorter suspension units and custom-built trail, often designed to take a smaller diameter front wheel. Prices range from about $300 for a simple and straightforward leading-link replacement fork to more than $1100 for top-quality leading-link forks complete with 15 in. spoked

wheel and tubless car tyre. A Dutch company, EML Techniek, specialises in producing high-quality sidecar conversion kits for Gold Wings. A range of five complete rolling chassis kits is available, comprising sidecar, rear wheel, front wheel, sidecar wheel, all tyres, and leading-link front forks. The sports version costs around $2300 and the touring model $2750. The owner still needs to supply the motorcycle frame, engine, seat, tank, electrics and lights, so the finished cost is by no means small. Nevertheless, British EML distributor Eddie Pinchbeck sells a steady 20 complete kits a year. The individual elements of the kit are also available separately, the most popular items being forks and wheels. EML 15 in. spoked wheels and tyres cost $190 front and $280 rear.

The advantage of the 15 in. wheels is that they can take standard car tyres which offer better grip, especially in wet weather, last longer and are cheaper to replace than motorcycle tyres. But the majority of Wing-based outfits still run on standard wheels for reasons of cost and most owners report excellent steering and very good high-speed handling. The standard GL disc brakes have proved to be well up to the task of stopping the added weight. Fuel consumption does not suffer too much, with most owners reporting 35 to 40 (Imperial) mpg in normal use.

Some owners use tricks like adding car valve springs to the front forks to stiffen the front suspension. Others use heavier-weight oil, aftermarket springs or air suspension conversion kits.

Owners report few problems from fitting sidecars to Gold Wings. In the UK, where sidecars are fitted on the left-hand side of the motorcycle, owners of early-model Wings found it virtually impossible to change the clutch cable because the sidecar got in the way. Honda redesigned the clutch operating mechanism on later models and eliminated the problem. In the US and

EML Techniek of Holland offers a range of purpose-built rolling chassis at prices from $2300 to $2750. The kits are expensive but well-made and include special wheels, tyres and forks

Continental Europe, fitting a sidecar on the right obscured the oil level sight window, but the introduction of dipsticks by a variety of accessory suppliers got rid of that problem, too.

One of the factors that inhibits even more Gold Wing owners from hitching a sidecar to their machines is the feeling that they would lose the pleasures of leaning the solo bike into curves. Mind you, I've been with one or two sidecar pilots who never let a minor factor like a sidecar prevent them from leaning into bends anyway, but that's another story. However, back about 1981, a California-based company launched the Equalean, a sidecar designed to lean with the motorcycle into corners. It set new standards for cornering performance in sidecar outfits and gave the avowed solo rider extra seating capacity without sacrificing too much in the way of handling. The Equalean has since become a firm favourite with Wing-owning sidecar fans, with several in evidence at Wing Ding.

Those who criticise the Gold Wing in solo form on the grounds of its weight and lack of cornering clearance are usually quick to admit its suitability as a sidecar machine. More and more Wing-based outfits appear on the roads each year. And, with sophisticated sidecars like the Equalean and others available, the Wing Nut can choose a sidecar that complements his or her motorcycle as much as any fairing, trailer or saddlebags would.

EML leading-link front forks fitted to a GL1100 at the 1982 British Treffen. The 15-inch spoked wheel carries a Uniroyal car tyre. This outfit also features an LPG gas conversion

7 The specials

This Dresda-framed GL1000 endurance racer (*below*) was the brainchild of Honda UK Ltd executive Ken Hull. The K1 model lapped the Isle of Man TT course in the hands of Hugh Evans (pictured here) at an average speed in the high 90s. Today, it's a street-legal café racer with 155 mph potential

A 'special' among Gold Wings is a special among specials and thus must be very special indeed. Since few Wing owners ride absolutely stock bikes, and since the customising permutations using bolt-on goodies are almost infinite, it follows that few Gold Wings are identical. Well, that's what I told myself when I parked my borrowed brown Aspencade in the multi-storey car park at Wing Ding in Steamboat Springs a couple of years ago. 'My' Aspencade was on loan from American Honda and therefore was box stock. The car park was almost empty when I parked there early one morning. By evening the place was full of Wings, about a third of them brown Aspencades and half of those box stock. It seems they were so new the owners hadn't had time to bolt on any goodies before heading for Wing Ding. Fancy finding *your* box stock Aspencade in among 50 other box stock Aspencades? The only thing that makes it easier than finding needles in haystacks is that at least Aspencades carry licence plates.

There must be hundreds of Gold Wing specials, maybe thousands. Virtually every Wing is a little bit special, so the problem becomes one of

The most special Wing of
them all—the futuristic
'feet forward' Phasar
(*above*) costs $3200 if
you add your own engine,
wheels and electrics. What
would the Honda designers
say? A GL1000 or 1100
engine is squeezed
between a strong
latticework of mild steel
(*left*). Fuel consumption
is in the 64–70 mpg range

This K1-based endurance racer (*below*) backed by the Swiss Honda importer was entered in a number of European long-distance events in 1976. *Der Grüne Blitz* (*opposite, top*) is the unique creation of Walter Knapp (*bottom*) of Albuquerque, New Mexico. Finished in deep metallic green, it features a 1976 GL1000 engine in an Electra Glide frame with Harley accessories

definition. If we define 'special' as 'significantly different from stock by means other than the addition of aftermarket accessories' then that narrows the field somewhat. Russ Collins' Wing-based dragster is certainly special by any definition. But by far and away the most radical road-going, Wing-based special I have come across to date is the Phasar, a product of the inventive mind of engineer and designer Malcolm Newell, who brought the world the successful Mini Marcos kit car and the revolutionary Quasar motorcycle.

I first met Malcolm when he was trying to get Quasar off the ground. If you have never even seen photographs of Quasar in the motorcycle press, let me describe it briefly here. It is a wedge-shaped touring motorcycle with a very long wheelbase within which lie the power unit, the rider and passenger. The device is more of a two-wheeled car than the Gold Wing can claim to be, because it has a roof connecting the steeply raked windscreen with a trunk or boot behind the passenger's head. Rider and passenger recline in racing-car fashion. The result is a light motorcycle with a low drag coefficient and a very low centre of gravity with excellent handling and roadholding. The original Quasar was powered by a Reliant 850 cc watercooled engine producing a mere 40 bhp. Yet on open roads it ran away and hid from my Honda CB750. The 80-bhp version launched not long before production ceased must have been phenomenal to ride.

My first question to Malcolm when I saw the Quasar was why didn't he use a Gold Wing engine instead. He said he wanted the bike to be all-British, and anyway he would have difficulty getting a guaranteed supply of Gold Wing engines from Honda. With the introduction of Phasar, he has obviously reconciled himself to the impossibility of the former condition and found an

ideal way around the latter. Phasar is a kit of parts—a near-complete rolling chassis—to which the rider must add his own Gold Wing engine and one or two ancilliaries.

The end result is certainly original: a 130 mph luxury tourer with a touring range of 1000 miles between fill-ups, averaging 65 (Imperial) mpg, offering a high degree of weather protection for rider and passenger, hot and cold air flow, more luggage space than even my wife could begin to use, and the handling and roadholding to outpace a 900 Ducati. There's even an integral tent as a optional extra! Sounds impressive, so it must cost the earth, right? Not really. If you supply your own engine, gearbox, rear wheel and electrics, and bolt the whole thing together yourself (a weekend job, Malcolm assures me), you can have a new Phasar for $3200 (£2130 including VAT). That's a lot less than some owners spend customising a Wing. Whether it's good value or not depends on whether you can live with the looks and how much you value function in a touring motorcycle.

The Phasar challenges conventional motorcycle design everywhere you look. The chassis comprises what could best be described as a double-A ladder framework, with one A-frame placed vertically above the other. The tapered end of the top frame points forward, the tapered end of the bottom frame rearward. Two more vertical A-frames separate the top and bottom members at front and rear. Between this latticework, with its crankcase under the rider's seat, is sandwiched an engine from a GL1000 or GL1100. The engine acts as a structural member, bearing much of the load on the chassis. The frame is made of thick-walled 16-gauge mild steel, $1\frac{1}{8}$ in. in diameter, circular in section, and MIG welded. No section of the frame spans more than 8 in. without support.

The owner of this Harleyesque Wing did a neat job of shoehorning the GL engine into a Super Glide (?) frame. How many Wing owners would have bought Harley if the American bikes had engines this good?

'Durability was a major consideration,' says Malcolm, 'so we didn't go overboard with lightweight tubing or material that was difficult to weld.' The Phasar still weighs much the same as a stock Gold Wing.

In front of the engine sits a $3\frac{1}{2}$-gallon fuel tank, and in front of that is a swinging-arm carrying a hub-centre steering system designed especially for this machine. Malcolm looked at the only other commercially available hub-centre system, the Difazio, and found it relied on too small a kingpin for his liking, so he designed a completely new system which uses a spherical joint in the centre of the axle. Among the advantages claimed for his system are bearings that run at lower speeds and thus present fewer sealing problems. It also has a second spherical joint 20 in. above the axle and the two form what is effectively the Phasar's steering head—the biggest in all of motorcycling.

The advantages of hub-centre steering are that the steering head does not support the weight of the motorcycle as in conventional telescopic fork systems; there is no nose-dive under even the heaviest of braking; the steering is light because the frictional forces are reduced; suspension units are free to perform their duty without also being responsible for keeping the wheel in line; and torsional rigidity is greatly improved. A hub-centre system in total also uses fewer components than are in even a single Gold Wing fork leg. And because the steering head no longer has to be braced by all the main frame tubes, the frame—and consequently seat height and centre of gravity—can be much lower than normal.

Malcolm claims that Honda has had its own hub-centre system for some time but has elected not to offer it for sale because conventional telescopic forks are selling so well. 'Why risk a major change when you're ahead?' seems to be

The GL-engined Hog stands out from the crowd at Steamboat Springs. This has to be one of the most imaginative specials around, along with *Der Grüne Blitz* and **Phasar**

the philosophy. No doubt Honda has other reasons for not putting the system into production, but since everyone who has ridden a bike with hub-centre steering has nothing but praise for the system it is a great shame that it has not yet been offered on the Wing. The current air fork with brace performs far better than such a highly stressed set-up might reasonably be expected to but a change could bring major benefits.

Malcolm's hub-centre steering offers adjustable trail between 2 and 3 inches. His own Phasar is set up with $2\frac{1}{2}$ in. and has 'very quick' steering, even with 24 in. handlebars. The rear suspension is conventional Honda, using the standard swinging arm. Brakes, hydraulics and wheels are standard Honda and tyres are Avon Venoms. The whole ensemble is sheathed in hand-laid fibreglass, comprising a very full fairing and an integral luggage box in the tail that will hold six safety helmets.

Weather protection is designed in from the outset. Rider and passenger sit inside rather than merely behind the fairing. The screen has a wiper as standard, and the radiator is positioned above the engine to duct warm air between rider and screen. Apart from keeping the rider warm on cold days (warm air is also ducted on to the hands and separate venturi outlets channel cool fresh air) the system is claimed to offset any turbulence which might otherwise occur around the fairing edges and thus keep rain out. 'You stay dry in the rain provided you don't stop!' says Malcolm.

He also reckons the Phasar boasts better handling and roadholding than virtually any sports bike, let alone any tourer. Ground clearance is nothing special—you can ground pieces of hardware if you try hard—but the roadholding is said to be phenomenal. Wheelbase is 64 in., overall width is 28

Opposite page **This California-plated K1 Wing, with a pair of twin-choke carbs hanging out way beyond the cylinders and a throaty-looking four-into-one exhaust, really looked The Business. Note the strange mix of neat alloy engine cowling and touring fairing**

Below **Behind the fairing of** *Der Grüne Blitz* **everything is polished to perfection. The owner keeps a selection of tapes of German marching music and gave me a blast of** *Deutschland Uber Ales* **or something very similar on his Panasonic deck!**

in., length is 86 in. and seat height is 16 in. for the rider and 18 for the passenger. The low seating position and the efficiency of the streamlining endow Phasar with remarkable fuel economy. One customer with a GL1000 version gets 64 (Imperial) mpg while a GL1100 owner reports 70 mpg. A frontal area claimed to be 20 per cent smaller than a normal Wing with touring fairing obviously pays dividends. The incredible touring range comes from two stainless steel long-range tanks, each holding six (Imperial) gallons, which fit inside the pair of 85 (yes, eighty-five!) litre saddlebags. The tanks are below seat height and come within the wheelbase, so their effect on handling and stability is minimal. And even with the tanks in place there's still more than 40 litres of luggage space available in each saddlebag. . . . And then there's that cavernous top box for lighter items. The low seat height makes visual comparison difficult, but the top of the Phasar's top box is the same height as the top of the back rest on an Aspencade.

What Malcolm Newell and his colleagues have produced is a single-minded solution to the problem of carrying two people and their baggage on two wheels over large distances without sacrificing comfort. At $3200 (£2130) it's an affordable solution, although you'll have to pay extra for the saddlebags ($180/£120 a pair) and the long-range tanks ($90/£60 a pair). An extra $105 (£70) buys you an integral tent which uses the motorcycle for support and provides accommodation for the motorcycle as well as the rider and passenger. It's all pretty clever stuff; God alone knows what might appear if Honda let the man loose in its design offices with a decent development budget.

The Gold Wing Executive was produced in Britain for Honda UK Ltd, the importer, by Rickman, better known for their fairings, luggage and café racers. Only 52 were built

Phasar may be the most radical Gold Wing 'special' on the streets, but it's not alone. A unique Dresda Gold Wing occasionally makes forays on British roads. It was originally the brainchild of Ken Hull, a manager with Honda (UK) Ltd, who built it from the remains of a crashed K1 Wing in 1976 to race in the Formula 1 TT in the Isle of Man and in the 500-mile Thruxton endurance race.

The standard frame was replaced with a duplex cradle frame from specialist frame-builders Dresda Autos of London who also made up a special four-into-one exhaust system. The standard swinging-arm was retained, 18 in. wheels fitted (the front was aluminium), standard Wing front forks and brakes used (with racing fluids) and S&W gas-filled shocks fitted at the rear.

Engine mods were relatively conservative. 'We tried nitriding the crank,' Ken says, 'but the drive gear is pressed on and the heat treatment tended to get it un-pressed!' So the connecting rods were shot-peened, the cylinder head skimmed and gas-flowed, racing cams from Russ Collins fitted, and the standard valves replaced with larger Honda CR competition valves. Pistons were standard. 'The top speed was over 155 mph and the handling was so good that the Wing could keep up with Charlie Williams on an RCB racing Honda,' Ken recalls.

The crank broke on its first outing at Thruxton. For the next outing, on the gruelling Isle of Man TT circuit, the gas shocks were replaced with S&W air shocks and TT veteran Hugh Evans took to the saddle. He lapped in practice at average speeds in the high 90s—a highly creditable achievement—but a broken oil-pressure relief valve spring put paid to his chances in the race.

Ken used his creation for sidecar racing, too, and finished third in a race at Brands Hatch on the first outing, with Jerry Raymond-Barker as his passenger. But eventually he sold it as a solo through London Honda dealer Mocheck who sold it several times over as a unique—and devastatingly quick—café racer for road use. Few owners, it seems, see any café racer potential in the Wing. A Swiss enthusiast regularly turns up at European Gold Wing rallies on a Wing-based café racer with a proprietary space-frame chassis. One or two others have been seen in basically standard form but with a few bolt-on café racer goodies. The rest have remained in touring mode.

Walter Knapp's Gold Wing *Der Grüne Blitz* (The Green Lightning) certainly counts as a special. This Wing enthusiast from Albuquerque, New Mexico, put a '76 GL1000 engine in a Harley Electra Glide frame, added a Harley front end, Monroe shocks, and Harley fairing, saddlebags and fenders. It's a beautifully executed custom (I'll always rue the day my film processing lab lost the roll with colour of Walter's bike on it) and Walter even stole the lead on the Phasar by adding two five-gallon (US) tanks which fit inside the saddlebags. And at least one enterprising US rider has shoe-horned a GL engine into a Harley Sportster frame to create a neat combination of mean-looking motorcycle and hassle-free engine—getting a boost in power, performance and smoothness to boot.

And then there are the factory or semi-factory specials—the Gold Wing LTD of 1976 in the USA and the Gold Wing Executive in Britain. Only 52 Executives were built—one for each week of the year—and they were devised by Honda (UK) Ltd, the British importer, to create interest in and a móre prestigious image for the Gold Wing. Finished in black, they featured a Rickman touring fairing and saddlebags, Lester spoked alloy wheels, and minor detail finish improvements.

8 Improving every year

It wasn't just the owners who busied themselves modifying the Gold Wing; Honda couldn't leave the machine alone either. In the nine years since its introduction, Honda has made subtle changes to the bike each year and on two occasions has radically revamped the machine. Without doubt, each year's model has been an improvement on the last and it is this continuous commitment to refining the basic concept that has made the very latest models into the best touring motorcycles currently available anywhere.

The original GL1000 K0 of 1975, with the design team led by Toshio Nozue, doesn't have a great deal in common with today's models other than that they share the same basic concept and the same engine configuration. But the frame, engine, wheels, seat, brakes, tyres, suspension and equipment levels have all taken quantum leaps forward in the intervening period. The '75 Wing, though, had an impressive specification for a touring bike. It was, for example, the first-ever Japanese shaft-driven motorcycle to be offered for sale in the West, the first Japanese motorcycle with triple disc brakes, the first Japanese four-stroke motorcycle with watercooling. It was also the heaviest volume production motorcycle in the world at 635 lb, barring the eccentric Harley-Davidson Electra Glide which virtually didn't exist outside the United States. It was the first modern motorcycle to have its cylinders cast into the crankcases, the first

First in a long line: the original 1975 GL1000 KO. Only 5000 were sold that year. Low-mileage examples in original condition are becoming collectors' items

to use inverted-toothed rubber belts to drive the camshafts, the first to use a contra-rotating alternator to compensate for the inherent torque reaction of a horizontally opposed engine. The Wing certainly had its share of innovatory ideas.

Basically the engine was a four-stroke horizontally opposed watercooled four with single overhead camshafts operating two valves per cylinder. It had a bore of 72 and a stroke of 61.4 mm for a displacement of 999 cc. Compression ratio was 9.2 to 1, carburetion was by four Keihin 32 mm constant-velocity butterfly-throttle units. The exhaust system was a four-into-two with a crossover pipe in front of the rear wheel. Power output was a claimed 80 bhp at 7500 rpm. Top speed depended on who was testing the bike but 122 mph was common. Wheelbase was 61 in., seat height 31.5 in., ground clearance 5.5 in. The frame was a heavy duplex cradle of tubular steel. The steering head rake was 28 degrees and the steering trail 4.7 in.

The gearbox was a five-speeder operating through a wet multiplate clutch. The ratios were 14.52:1, 9.92:1, 7.74:1, 6.37:1 and 5.45:1 (top). Final drive was, of course, by shaft to a crown wheel and pinion with a ratio of 3.40:1. The electrical system comprised a 300W alternator, battery and coil ignition, a 12V 20 amp-hour battery and 50/40W headlight. Performance was stunning, considering the machine's all-up weight: standing quarter-mile in 12.92 seconds with a terminal speed of 105.5 mph in the quarter and a top speed of 122 mph.

For 1976, under the leadership of Einosuke Miyachi, Honda kept the Wing virtually unchanged except for minor cosmetic differences and one important

Even in 1974, Honda had visions of a faired Gold Wing, but it never went any further until the launch of the GL1100 Interstate in 1980

mechanical improvement. The '75 models offered no provision for greasing the driveshaft splines. Owners had to disassemble the rear end of the motorcycle every 6000 miles to repack the splines with grease. Most GL owners equated shaft drive with zero maintenance and there were some cases of drive-train failure through lack of proper lubrication. So far 1976 Honda installed an external grease nipple to make the task much less of a chore. The nipple was retrofitted free of charge to '75 Wings by Honda dealers. The '76 K1 model also featured a wiper on the oil level sight window, a carburettor link guard, two helmet holders and new coachlining. The same year also saw the launch of the limited-edition LTD with gold wheels and a special 'prestige' high-grade finish.

But 1977 saw the launch of the K2 model, under team leader Masaru Shira-kura who had developed the 125–175 cc engine range, with numerous detail improvements. It featured a stylish new paint job with more pinstriping, a slightly more comfortable seat, and tapered roller bearings in the steering head instead of ball bearings as previously. The exhaust header pipes got chrome covers and the triangular upper engine mounting brackets went from black gloss to chrome. The fuel tank was specially treated to prevent rust and efforts were made to reduce mechanical noise still further.

The first big changes came in 1978 with the launch of the GL1000 K3. Project leader Masahiro Senbu set out to tackle some of the earlier complaints from riders and testers about a lack of low-end and mid-range power, ride comfort, seat comfort and wet-weather braking. The Wing also received its first real styling face-lift and looked better as a result. There was a new paint job in a deep and lustrous black, highlighted by gold pinstriping. Honda's new invention of the day, Comstar wheels, graced the new model in place of the

For 1976, the K1 sported minor detail changes like more pin-striping and chrome-plated upper rear engine brackets

traditional spoked alloy wheels of earlier Wings. The much-criticized black exhaust was replaced by a new all-chrome set-up which looked better and had a throatier yet still subdued growl. The dual seat gained more padding and a step in its centre. The headlight was now a halogen unit. The dummy tank top now hinged backwards rather than forwards and was finished in imitation grained leather and carried a pod for three instruments: fuel and temperature gauges and a voltmeter. And the emergency kickstart lever made its exit. The most radical changes lay inside the engine, however. Smaller carburettors, less radical valve timing and greater ignition advance gave a flatter power curve and boosted low- and mid-range power at the expense of top-end performance—a trade-off most Wing owners were more than happy to make.

The Keihin carbs now had 31 mm throats rather than 32 mm. Intake timing was reduced by 15 degrees. The intake valves now opened at 5 degrees before top dead centre and closed at 35 degrees after bottom dead centre, compared with 5 degrees BTDC and 50 degrees ABDC previously. Exhaust timing had 10 degrees less duration, beginning at 40 degrees before bottom dead centre and finishing at 5 degrees after top dead centre, compared with 50 degrees BBDC and 5 degrees ATDC previously. Ignition advance remained at 10 degrees up to 800 rpm as before, but increased to a maximum of 25.5–27 degrees compared with 23–24.5 degrees. Power was down slightly to 78 bhp but maximum torque of 60 ft lb was now produced at 5550 rpm instead of 6500 rpm previously.

The effect on top end was noticeable. Standing quarter-mile time was slower at 13.38 seconds (12.92 seconds previously) with a terminal speed of 98.9 mph (105 mph before) and top speed was down 2 mph at 120 mph. But there was more usable power in the mid-range and fifth-gear throttle roll-ons brought

In 1976 the US got this limited-edition Wing, the LTD, with gold-anodized wheels and an upmarket finish

results without the need for downshifting, despite the fact that overall gear ratios remained unchanged. Hills had less effect on the bike in top gear and overtaking could be accomplished more quickly and safely. The K3 did suffer, however, from a slight hesitancy off idle which may have been due to carburetion changes to meet American Environmental Protection Agency rules. Switching from the stock Nippon Denso plugs to Champion A-8Y-MC improved the position slightly and alleviated the machine's in-bred cold-bloodedness when starting.

Another internal engine mod was the addition of locating pins in the piston grooves for the oil ring. This was to prevent the gaps in the rings on the left-side cylinders from being at the bottom of the pistons. What used to happen as a result of this on earlier models was that oil would seep past the ring while the bike was parked on its side stand. It would then get into the combustion chambers and burn—visibly—for a few miles. Not any more. And a blow-by recirculation system was added.

The Hy-Vo primary chain on the K3 sprouted a spring-loaded tensioner to further reduce primary drive noise; earlier models just had a fixed chain guide. And the new exhaust system meant that access to the clutch was much easier than before. Suspension travel up front had been increased by 1 in., the front fork springs were 6 mm longer, chamfers were cut in the bottom of each fork leg to channel oil between the tubes and sliders in a bid to reduce static friction, and the damping rate had been altered. This brought some improvement but was still a long way off perfection. At the rear end, FVQ shock absorbers were introduced without noticeable improvement.

My road test of the K3 in *Hondaway* magazine contained the following:

The 1979 models had a lustrous black finish, all-chrome exhausts with a throatier note, a tank-top instrument pod and a new seat

'Passenger comfort was inhibited not by the saddle but by the harshness of the rear suspension. Gold Wings have long been criticised for stiff springing and damping, made necessary by the machine's considerable weight and the need to maximise ground clearance. It's fine on billiard-smooth surfaces—just like riding on air. But as soon as the road gets bumpy the ride gets very choppy and the passenger comes off worst. Two passengers found the bike uncomfortable for this reason. The rider doesn't suffer quite so badly, but the front fork is fairly firm and the ride could be more comfortable. Owners who fit accessory shock absorbers report favourably on the improvement, so perhaps 1980 will see the Wing fitted with air forks and shocks at the factory.' Whether that was brilliant prophecy or an informed guess I can no longer remember!

Wet-weather braking had been a cause for complaint. So much so, in fact, that rider complaints caused an investigation by the US Department of Transportation. So the K3 was fitted with the front discs and calipers from the CB750F2 which were lighter and performed slightly better in the rain. Another safety boost was the fitting of really loud twin horns which were light years ahead of the anaemic single horn which caused much embarrassment to K1 and K2 Wing riders.

One safety-related matter that wasn't cleared up on the K3 was a mysterious high-speed weave that I had experienced on several Wings and which was reported also by other riders but which was never highlighted, as far as I can recall, in other road tests. A weave would start from the rear end at 100 mph (on the K2) and 110 mph (on the K3) and bring a mild wobble in the handlebars which grew progressively worse as speed increased. On several occasions I had to fight hard to slow the machine down without getting into a

GLC 77T was the K3 test bike that caused me one enormous problem: I'd just spent more than $5000 dollars that week on a new BMW and found I preferred the (considerably cheaper) Honda . . .

tank-slapper. The best cure was to grip the bars very tightly, slide back along the dualseat and lower your weight further on to the dummy tank. At least the sensation came 10 mph further up the scale on the K3 but it was still unsettling. Tyre pressures were normal in every case and the weaves were not provoked by road irregularities, cats' eyes or white lines.

One of the ironic things about the K3—or the KZ as it was known in the UK—with its attractive instrument pod was the fact that by this time the Wing was becoming quite popular as a touring mount in Europe. But the designers were still thinking of the American market. Few serious European touring riders travel any distance without a tank-top bag to carry their heaviest luggage, to minimise the effect on handling. But tank bags totally obscured the three little instruments from the rider's view! It was of little real consequence: the engine never overheated and the fuel gauge was hopelessly inaccurate.

The KZ remained virtually unchanged as the K4 for 1979 under Ryo Nashimoto as the factory concentrated on radical changes for the '80 models. The levers became anodized black, the circular brake fluid reservoir became translucent and rectangular, and the direction indicators went rectangular too. American models got the 60/55W quartz halogen headlight that had been winning friends in Europe for some time. The front brake discs were changed again to one-piece units, and the tail light was all-new and featured twin bulbs.

Then 1980 was the milestone year for the Gold Wing. Honda unveiled what was virtually an all-new motorcycle from stem to stern. The five-year-old 1000 cc engine had been replaced by an 1100 cc motor. The frame was new, and so

The first major change in Gold Wing design came in 1980 at the hands of Shuji Tanaka in the shape of the GL1100. It answered in one fell swoop complaints about the seat and suspension

was the suspension at long last. Detail changes abounded. The GL1100 represented a breakthrough for Honda in the touring motorcycle class, according to American Honda marketing executive Bob Doornbos. Ever since the introduction of the GL1000 the rival factories had been working hard to catch up, with bikes like the Suzuki GS1000, the Yamaha XS1100, Kawasaki Z1300 and BMW R100RT. The Gold Wing was in need of a facelift and in marketing terms at least it needed more engine displacement. The GL1100 delivered.

Honda's designers, under team leader Shuji Tanaka who was to head the Gold Wing's development for the next five model years, more than met those criteria and in doing so they eliminated in one fell swoop virtually all the shortcomings that had bothered riders ever since 1975.

Mr Tanaka was a frame designer with Honda before he took over as project leader on the Gold Wing. After leaving university he worked for a company called Martin in Kobe, Japan, where he designed the frame for a two-stroke 250 using a British Villiers engine. The company folded, so the young Mr Tanaka joined the Tohatsu company where he designed the frame for a motorcycle called the GB90. Tohatsu also went to the wall, ironically a victim of the increasing success of a company called Honda. If you can't beat 'em, join 'em, and so Mr Tanaka joined Honda in 1961 as a frame designer. Among his many successes were the CB90, CB110, CB125 single, CB125 and CD185 twins, the C50 and C70 step-throughs, TL125 and TL250 trials bikes, the RTL300 competition trials bike, MT250 trail bike, XL185 and XL200, the

The 1980 GL1100 DX-B as it was known in the UK, or Interstate in the US. Suddenly, Honda had produced the sort of touring machine that Wing Nuts had been building for themselves for five years

CBX1000 and—more recently—the VF750S and VF750C; he was also partly responsible for the popular VF750F. So he came to the GL1100 with a first-class track record, and it is hardly surprising that he paid close attention to the handling and ride of Honda's prestigious touring machine.

According to Mr Tanaka, the designers chose to raise the Gold Wing's capacity for two reasons: to cope with the added weight of fairings, saddlebags and all the accessories being bolted and strapped to Gold Wings from New York to LA; and to eliminate the problem of broken crankshafts which had been reported from Europe. 'It seemed that some European riders were riding their Gold Wings flat out for long periods, and this had led to a small number of crankshaft breakages,' Mr Tanaka says. 'The increased capacity and the general strenghthening of the GL motor put an end to those breakages. Also, when we launched the six-cylinder CBX in 1978, aimed at Europeans who wanted to ride flat out, we were able to cast the Gold Wing more directly in a touring role.'

The extra displacement came from boring out the cylinders by 3 mm to 75 mm while the stroke remained the same at 61.4 mm. The result was that capacity was up from 999 cc to 1085 cc. The rest of the motor was beefed up to cope with the extra power—now up to a claimed 81 bhp from 78 bhp—even though the GL1000 components could have coped comfortably. A new crankshaft had larger big-end and main bearing journals, the Hy-Vo primary

Shuji Tanaka, the frame designer who went on to head the design team for the GL1100 and eventually the GL1200. The 1100 had a stronger crankshaft to eliminate breakages caused by flat-out riding in Europe

chain was wider with an improved tensioner, the clutch was larger and stronger, and the gearbox output shaft was heftier by 3 mm. All-new camshafts increased the inlet valve lift and the valve timing was revised to give more power. The carburettors were new aluminium Keihin 30 mm constant velocity units designed to boost low-end and mid-range response. Carburettors on the original K1 had been 32 mm diameter and those on the K3 were 31 mm. The old ignition points were finally replaced by electronic ignition with both a normal centrifugal advancer and a new vacuum advancer which adjusted the ignition advance to suit engine load and made for cleaner running at all engine speeds.

The new elctronic ignition system was mounted at the rear of the engine and necessitated a lenghening of the frame and a consequent extension of the wheelbase from an already long 60.8 in to a staggering 63.2 in. This in turn allowed seat height to be reduced slightly from 31.5 to 31.3 in and the long wheelbase combined with a steep rake (29 degrees 10 minutes) and a long trail (5.3 in) to give exceptional straight-line stability at all speeds. Gone was the weave at 100–110 mph of the K2 and K3.

Another major and long-overdue improvement came in the suspension. Air suspension was now standard front and rear and transformed the Wing not only into a most luxurious tourer but also into a much better back-road handler. The front fork tubes were 2 mm thicker than previously at 39 mm to reduce flexing. Both fork legs had coil springs but much of the support was now provided by air pressure. Both legs were linked via a common single air valve on top of the right-hand fork leg. Friction-reducing twin Syntallic bushings were fitted in each leg to help cut sliding friction to about half what it would be with all-metal bushings. As a result, the static friction which had plagued the

Next pages Cutaway drawings reveal (*top left*) the GL1000 engine and transmission, the efficient lubrication system (*bottom left*), the fuel and engine cooling arrangements (*top right*) and the disc brake mechanism (*bottom right*)

Below Not a lot you can say about this, unless you read Japanese, but these are some of the engineers' notes during the development of the GL1000

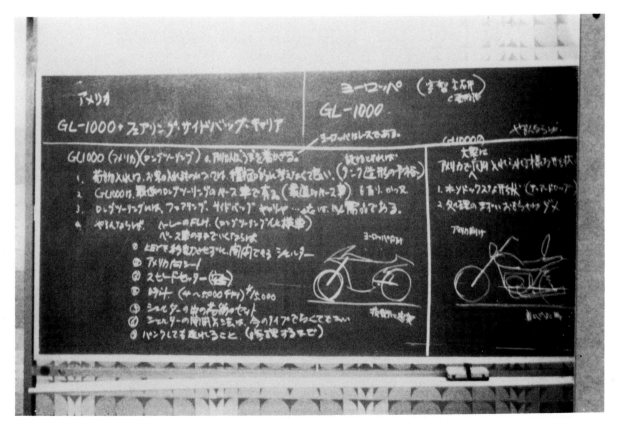

GL1000 ENGINE & DRIVE SYSTEMS

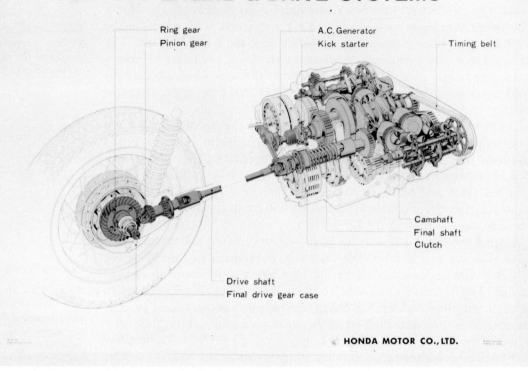

Ring gear / Pinion gear — A.C.Generator / Kick starter — Timing belt — Camshaft / Final shaft / Clutch — Drive shaft / Final drive gear case — HONDA MOTOR CO., LTD.

GL1000 OIL LUBRICATION SYSTEM

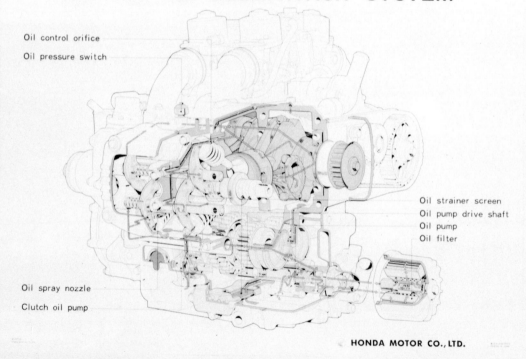

Oil control orifice / Oil pressure switch — Oil strainer screen / Oil pump drive shaft / Oil pump / Oil filter — Oil spray nozzle / Clutch oil pump — HONDA MOTOR CO., LTD.

GL1000 FUEL & COOLING SYSTEMS

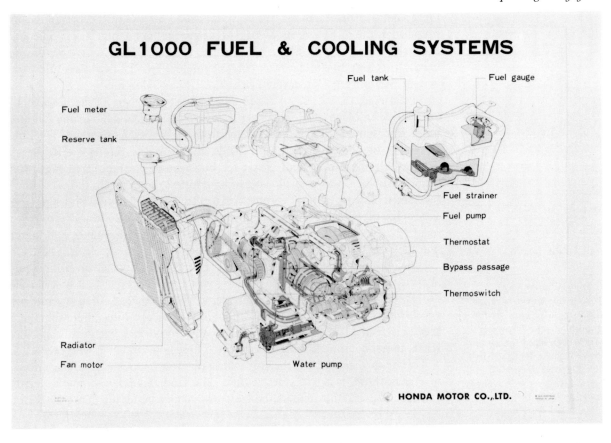

Fuel meter
Reserve tank
Fuel tank
Fuel gauge
Fuel strainer
Fuel pump
Thermostat
Bypass passage
Thermoswitch
Radiator
Fan motor
Water pump

HONDA MOTOR CO., LTD.

GL1000 DISC BRAKE MECHANISM

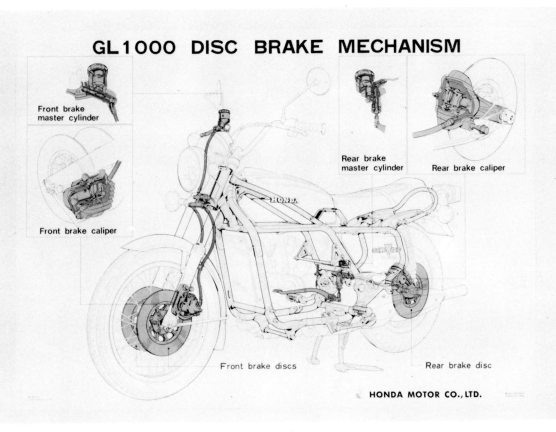

Front brake master cylinder
Front brake caliper
Rear brake master cylinder
Rear brake caliper
Front brake discs
Rear brake disc

HONDA MOTOR CO., LTD.

Gold Wing's front forks for five years was gone for good. Recommended air pressure in the forks was 14–21 psi. At 14 psi the fork action was supple and extremely comfortable without being mushy. Higher pressure gave better ride height, less fork dive under heavy braking and still gave a first-class ride—the best in the touring motorcycle world.

At the rear, too, a pair of oil/air-filled shock absorbers brought a magic-carpet ride in place of the much-criticised conventional coil-sprung damper units. Recommended pressures ranged from 29–42 psi. At the lower level the rider was literally floating on air while at 40 psi the ride was still plenty comfortable for a rider and passenger but ground clearance was improved slightly and there was no wallowing or twitchiness. The wheels, too, were new: reversed Comstars in black with polished alloy highlights and with wider rims shod with tubeless tyres for the first time: a 110/90–19 front and 130/90–17 rear. They promised better grip, better wet weather performance and better mileage. They delivered on all three counts.

What else did people want changed? The seat? The 1100 had an all-new seat in true custom king-and-queen style. It was a vast improvement and had its own three-position fore and aft adjustment. This needed an Allen key and was a little fiddly to adjust. A lot of folk thought it was a great idea, but others said they preferred a flatter seat on which the rider could slide backwards and forwards to get comfortable on a long trip. There's no pleasing everybody. . . .

The stepped seat wasn't the only concession to what owners had been doing to Wings those past five years, either. The front fender was now a deeply valenced Harleyesque item in fibreglass which did a better job than ever before

The distinctive cleft rocker box cover is an obvious difference from the older 1000 cc model. All Wings lived up to their luxurious image by keeping the engine oil inside where the designers intended. No leaks

of keeping the road dirt away from bike and rider. An attractive new paint scheme graced the 1100, a rich metallic wine-red with gold lining. The dummy tank sides no longer folded down and the top flipped up in two parts, allowing the rider to reach the fuel filler without disturbing a tank-top bag. Nice touch. And of the three gauges that graced the tank top of the K3, the voltmeter had disappeared and the fuel and temperature gauges were relocated on top of the speedometer and revcounter. European models wore US-style handlebars with an eight-inch rise, instead of the Europe-only flatter bars that had been fitted to previous models. They were comfortable up to 90 mph but not beyond on the unfaired bike. But past experience told Honda that most riders—about 85 per cent of Wing riders—would fit some kind of fairing.

The new Wing promised to last even longer than the old, too. Plastic was used extensively: both fenders, sidepanels, dummy tank and seat base. And the new exhaust system no longer had that rust trap of a balance box in front of the rear wheel. The exhaust note was louder than that of the K1 and K2 but on a par with the K3. Other changes included new horns that were even louder than the K3's, fuel tank capacity increased from 4.2 Imperial gallons to 4.4 (5.3 US gallons), a new and more powerful three-phase alternator, a spare power point for accessories up to 60W (5 amps), a warning light in the revcounter for low air pressure in the rear shocks, and a fuel gauge that made more than a passing stab at accuracy. Overall gear ratios were new, too: 12.84:1, 8.56:1, 6.61:1, 5.47:1 and 4.67:1 (top). The brakes had new discs (the front 1 mm smaller than the rear) that were immensely powerful, fade-free, pulse-free and totally predictable.

This single valve on the right fork leg of the 1980 GL1100 served both front fork legs. Recommended pressures ranged from 14 to 21 psi

The net result of Honda's redesign of the Gold Wing was to make it the most comfortable, the most relaxing and probably the most dependable touring motorcycle in the world. It rode better, handled better, looked better and *was* better than any of its predecessors. Never mind the fact that the weight was up to 589 lb dry or 636 lb with a full tank; what's a few extra pounds between friends?

But in the same year of 1980 Honda went further than this. They introduced their own full-dress touring version of the Wing, dubbed the Interstate in the USA and the GL1100DX (or De Luxe) in Europe. Here was the complete tourer, all dressed up and ready to go to the other side of the world: just add rider, toothbrush, fuel and credit cards. The Interstate was Honda's belated attempt to attract a little of the considerable sums of money being lavished on the aftermarket suppliers of fairings, saddlebags and radios. For an extra £400 in Britain you got a first-class touring fairing, two 36-litre saddlebags and a 49-litre travel trunk or top case, all colour-matched to the bike. Also included were engine protection bars which intruded a little too much on the rider's shin-space at a standstill and were the cause of much bruising and cursing, a from-the-saddle headlight adjuster, an adjustable windscreen, and a clever shield over the instruments to prevent distracting reflections in the screen at night. The Interstate was a bargain few tourers could afford to miss and the entire year's production sold out in every world market without satisfying demand. All the extra equipment added 100 lb to the Wing's not inconsiderable weight. In fact, the factory even added it's own weight to the front forks behind the fairing to compensate for the weight lost from the steering axis when the headlight was relocated into the frame-mounted fairing. Plans to cease

Detail improvements for 1981 included self-cancelling indicators, yet another new seat, finger-operated seat adjustment, and a higher maximum pressure limit on the rear shocks

production of the unfaired version were dropped following strong protests from the major American fairing manufacturers who saw their sales threatened.

In 1981 the changes were few but significant nonetheless. Efforts were made to counter carburettor surging. Tyres became US Dunlops. The seat was slightly altered in shape and the fore-aft movement was now controlled by a simple finger latch—no tools needed. A lot of riders had complained that the rear suspension still bottomed out with a full load at 42 psi, so the maximum air pressure limit was increased to 57 psi. The screen blade on the fairing was changed to a scratch-resistant polycarbonate. The warning lights were covered by a new tinted shield. And self-cancelling indicators were fitted for the first time since the 1974 prototype. This was a sophisticated system controlled by a micro-processor which was governed by the three variables of speed, steering angle and steering duration. At more than 23 mph, the indicators would self-cancel after five seconds. Below 23 mph, they would cancel after 120 metres.

The 1100 featured an audible warning device to remind the rider to cancel the indicators. Over 40 mph they beeped, under 40 they clicked—except in the UK where beeping indicators had just been withdrawn from new motorcycles because the sound was too similar to the audible warning of Britain's pedestrian crossings and the noise had been confusing blind pedestrians; I kid you not. Optional extras included an AM-FM radio and rider intercom at $450, a voltmeter, quartz clock and air temperature gauge. The radio was not sold in the UK, partly because its price would have been prohibitive and partly because Honda (UK) Ltd, the importers, had reservations about the use of radios and cassette decks on motorcycles.

The 1981 Interstate will be remembered by many shins for the bruising they received from the engine bars. Options included stereo radio, cassette deck and rider intercom

The Interstate was the direct result of liaison between American Honda and the Gold Wing Road Riders Association. Honda said 'Look, this is what we are planning to do, what do you, the riders, think?'. Perhaps that is why the Interstate ended up like a factory version of all the owner-modified Wings already plying the American highways. In any event, Honda and the riders were both winners.

Honda continued to modify and refine the basic Wing and Interstate for 1982. The saddlebag lids were redesigned to reduce the risk of water penetration; the passenger footrests were new, to reduce vibration (what vibration?); the engine protection bars were foreshortened and now no one but a fool could bang his or her shins on them; and the dual-piston brake calipers from the CB900 joined the fray. Third, fourth and fifth gear ratios were increased to lower engine revolutions still further and boost fuel economy. Wheel diameters changed also, the front going down from 19 in. to 18 in. and the rear from 17 in. to 16 in. Tyre widths were increased to 120/90–18 at the front and a chunky 140/90–16 at the rear. The new rear tyre was designed to give 14,000 to 15,000 miles of wear before replacement—a considerable improvement on the 1975 model. The 5-amp accessory take-off point was uprated to 10 amps.

But the biggest change for '82 was the introduction of yet another new model, the GL1100 Aspencade. This was a luxury version of the established Interstate and was visually differentiated by a striking two-tone brown or two-tone grey paint scheme. Standard features included an on-board air compressor mounted in the dummy tank and operated from a pushbutton console on the tank top. The system could only be operated with the ignition

Opposite page, *top* **The 1982 Aspencade offered everything the touring rider could possibly want, including a vanity mirror in the top-case for vain riders/passengers. It was available in two-tone combinations of grey or brown and was simply the most luxurious Wing yet. Like the 1982 Interstate (*bottom*), its engine bars were altered to reduce shin wear**

Below **Minor improvements continued on the 1982 Wing, with wider tyres, new passenger footrests, dual-piston brake calipers, altered gear ratios and smaller wheel diameters**

switch on 'park' to prevent riders altering pressures on the move. The Aspencade also wore the ventilated disc brakes first seen on the CBX-B, still with dual-piston calipers. The seat was new, the new backrest incorporated two neat zippered pouches at either side for easy passenger access on the move, and the travel trunk featured a vanity mirror and map case in the lid. The AM-FM stereo radio was fitted as standard, complete with a station search facility that automatically switched to the next receivable station down the waveband at the touch of a button. Options now included a cassette player, a 40-channel CB radio, a voice-actuated intercom system, and rider/passenger headsets.

With so many changes in only two years, most folk expected the Wing to remain pretty much the same for 1983. Nobody told Honda. Instead, the '83 models sported 11-spoke cast alloy wheels, a V4-style alloy front fork brace, a left thumb-operated choke lever, a removeable rear fender section for easier wheel removal, flatter footrests (which were adjustable for passengers), a box-section swingarm—and that was just for starters. Honda R&D pointed out, incidentally, that the new wheels were in response to customer preference and that the Comstars were every bit as strong.

All the '83s got Honda's Torque Reactive Anti-Dive Control (TRAC) system which uses front brake torque reaction to activate and modulate anti-dive force. The TRAC units are four-way adjustable for different degrees of dive resistance. Also common to all models in '83 was Honda's unified brake

The 1983 Aspencade offered an LCD instrument panel, TRAC anti-dive braking, unified braking system, yet another new seat, altered suspension, higher gearing, and other detail mods

system by which the foot pedal applies direct pressure to the right *front* disc and activates the rear disc through a pressure control valve. The handlebar lever controls the left front disc only. The system is designed to prevent premature rear wheel lock-up under heavy braking while still allowing a constant ratio of front:rear braking until the rear brake's control valve comes into play.

The Aspencade and Interstate had their travel trunks moved back 30 mm and up 25 mm to boost passenger comfort and the Interstate's backrest was enlarged for the same reason. The dual seat was lengthened by 30 mm and the rider's portion narrowed by 30 mm to reduce the passenger's leg splay. The engine guards were altered again to allow even more room for the rider's shins than in '82. Overall gearing was raised by 8 per cent to get even better fuel mileage and reduce engine wear still further. Then, to compensate, first gear was reduced from 2.50:1 to 2.64:1. The gearing changes made high-speed cruising even less of a strain but meant that top-gear acceleration was once again a little sluggish below 60 mph. Changing down to fourth became a prerequisite for fast overtaking at such speeds, just as it was with the K1 and K2.

The front forks received further attention. The third stage of fork springing was stiffened 10 per cent and compression damping increased 7 per cent in a bid to reduce the risk of bottoming. The springs in the rear shocks were made 50 per cent stiffer than before and the shocks now relied on the coil springs more than on air in an effort to reduce static friction caused by high air

The 1983 GL1100 shared with the Interstate and Aspencade the new 11-spoke cast alloy wheels, the front fork brace, TRAC anti-dive and unified braking. The inexorable programme of refinement continued

Honda's marketing men came up with this 1000-piece jigsaw puzzle in 1976 to give Wing Nuts something else to do while their bike was being serviced

pressure. The '83s could run with no air in the shocks and consequently the low air pressure warning light was no longer included. The Aspencade's on-board compressor could now be operated with the ignition switch at 'on' rather than 'park', with or without the engine running, and the pushbuttons were relocated from the tank top to the fork crown. The tank top had been saved yet again for tank-bag users.

The icing on the Aspencade cake for '83 was an all-new liquid crystal instrumentation display. LCD bar graphs illustrate engine revs in conjunction with a digital rpm display. The speedometer was also digital, and LCDs also kept the rider informed of fuel level, engine temperature, suspension pressures, distance travelled this trip and distance still to go. Bar graphs illustrated front and rear suspension air pressure. Amber and red lights warned the rider of impending service intervals (now 9000 miles apart).

The handlebar-mounted mute switch/signal-seeking switch for the radio was raised a fraction to avoid a clash with the dipswitch, and the self-cancelling indicator operating system was modified to eliminate a problem with the turn-angle sensor not always being activated and the signal not cancelling in certain circumstances.

Few motorcycles can have had such an active programme of model development. The Gold Wing was good to begin with; its continual refinement over the nine years to 1983 made it the undisputed leader in touring motorcycles. The '83 Aspencade seemed to offer the ultimate in luxury touring; what could possibly be added for '84? A touch more mid-range power? A mobile telephone? On-board word-processing for the executive on the move? Or maybe just a wider choice of colours?

The first hint that something more fundamental might be in the pipeline came in August 1982 when American Honda's Bob Doornbos told me that Honda was committed to the long-term future of the Gold Wing. 'In time, it may be very different to today's Wing, but there will always be a Gold Wing in the Honda range,' he said. The next hint came when we tried to interview Shuji Tanaka in Japan about his involvement in Wing design. The interview, we were told, would have to wait until after October 1983—the traditional time of year for announcing new models. What emerged for press scrutiny at the Tochigi test track was no mere face-lifted GL but essentially a whole new touring motorcycle that contrived successfully to look like the Wing we know and love.

9 The GL1200

Despite the alternative reasons advanced by Honda's engineers and designers for the introduction of the Gold Wing and its subsequent development, there can be little doubt that intense competition from other factories played the major role. The initial design stemmed from the fact that the CB750 Honda flagship had been overshadowed by newer, faster models from rival manufacturers. Similarly, the introduction of the GL1100 was as much a response to the Yamaha XS1100 and new models from other stables as it was a pure re-design exercise in itself. So when Yamaha wheeled out its latest frontal assault on Gold Wing sales, the V4 XVZ1200 Venture, in 1983, the ball was firmly back in Honda's court. The world's largest motorcycle manufacturer served up the GL1200A, a totally new Gold Wing in all but name.

The 1200 features a new engine, new frame, new wheels, new fairing, new luggage, new styling, new seat, new suspension and a whole array of new ideas designed to grant a new lease of life to a nine-year-old design. With Shuji Tanaka in charge of design for the fifth year running, the latest Wing fairly bristles with clever solutions to the age-old problem of making a large and heavy tourer feel and act like a much smaller and more nimble motorcycle.

Chassis modifications start with the wheels: the front is down to 16 in. in diameter from the 1100's 18 in., and the rear wheel is now an inch smaller at 15 in. The immediate result is an even lower centre of gravity and faster steering response. Then the steering head was lowered and moved farther back, the rake was increased from 29.2 degrees to 30 degrees and the trail reduced from 5.2 in. to 4.6 in. The swinging arm was lengthened by 2.2 in. and the engine moved forward in the frame by 2.5 in. Fork stanchion diameter was increased to 41 mm—a full 4 mm more than the original GL1000. The combined result of these changes is not only greatly improved handling but also a lightness and nimbleness on the move that belies the Aspencade's 790 lb wet weight. It's easier to ride in traffic than the 1100 and can be pushed further on twisting country roads.

Suspension has been modified slightly, with nearly 50 per cent more rebound damping at the rear end; compression damping has been reduced slightly at both ends and the springing stiffened front and rear. The result is more suspension travel all round. The adjustable air suspension (with on-board compressor on the Aspencade) endows the 1200 with a supremely comfortable highway ride and a new degree of tautness for sportier riding. The forward placement and slight uptilting of the engine also gives the new Wing more ground clearance than ever before. Wider tyres (130/90 front, 150/90 rear), Honda's TRAC anti-dive and unified front/rear braking systems, and the frame and suspension improvements make the latest Wing a far more realistic proposition for fast, safe riding on winding backroads.

The 1200 engine is virtually all-new, although visually not dissimilar to the

1100 unit. Capacity has been punched out to 1182 cc by increasing the stroke from 61.4 to 66 mm. The bore is fractionally larger at 75.5 mm. The cylinder heads feature a more efficient combustion chamber design, inlet valves that are 2 mm larger than before at 36 mm (exhaust valve diameter stays the same at 32 mm), altered valve timing and more valve lift. With new 32 mm Keihin constant-velocity carburettors, a 9:1 compression ratio and a new computer-controlled ignition system, the 1200 puts out a claimed 94 bhp at 7000 rpm and 10.7 kgm of torque at 5000 rpm compared with the 1100's 81 bhp at 7500 rpm and 9.2 kgm at 5500 rpm. The extra power and torque don't make the 1200 much of a sprinter: for one thing, the Aspencade version weighs a whopping 790 lb ready to roll; and the overall gearing has been raised by fitting a new 2.83 final drive. Internal gearing remains unaltered, and the smaller rear wheel at least partly makes up for the higher gearing, but the standing-start quarter-mile time of 13.3 seconds won't break any records. Rapid acceleration on the move requires downshifting to fourth or even third gear.

Other changes have been wrought inside the motor. A clever hydraulic arrangement operating on the rocker shafts maintains a constant tappet clearance which never needs adjustment. Hydraulics have also taken over the task of clutch operation, compensating automaticcally for any wear. A diaphragm spring has replaced the conventional coil springs of the GL1000 and GL1100, and the 1200's clutch gets an additional clutch plate. Lever pull remains light.

There's also a new radiator which has only two rows to the old one's three, so it's smaller and lighter and manages to do a better job of keeping engine temperatures low. The alternator output is 60W up on the 1100's at a powerful 360W to enable the bolt-on fans to bolt on more than ever before.

The all-new 1200 cc Gold Wing for 1984 came as a surprise to those who felt the 1983s were state-of-the-art tourers. Almost everything had changed for the better, but the stylists were careful to keep just enough of the old classic lines not to alienate their best customers

Visually, the overall impression is that the Wing has not changed too much. But the fairing on the Interstate and Aspencade models is all-new and does a better job than ever of protecting the rider from the elements. The screen is taller and the mirrors serve also to deflect wind from the rider's hands. The result is less buffeting and less wind noise. The travel trunk has been redesigned to provide more carrying capacity, a higher passenger backrest and new elbow rests! The saddlebags too are larger, with improved waterproof seals. Overall luggage capacity is now 25 per cent higher than the previous Aspencade and Interstate. The passenger footrests have been replaced by footboards, and the forward placement of the engine gives the rider's shins an easier time. The seat is new, too, and supremely comfortable.

The Aspencade gets a new stereo AM/FM radio and cassette player (a $900 option on the Interstate) with optional headsets ($100 a time). Other options include a CB radio transceiver ($325) and a remote-control audio handset for the passenger ($60). The radio/cassette is now mounted in the front of the fairing above the instruments rather than in the left fairing lower as before. The instruments themselves are all liquid-crystal displays, save the mechanical odometer. The tachometer graph of the 1983 model has been ditched in favour of a digital-only readout.

The 1200 was a satisfying achievement for Mr Tanaka, who had taken over as leader of the Gold Wing design team in 1979 to produce the first 1100 in 1980. 'Just about everything I hoped to do to the Gold Wing has been achieved

Ten years on and still going stronger than ever— the Gold Wing has confounded its critics, delighted its devotees, and opened up a whole new chapter in luxurious long-distance motorcycle travel. A third of a million motorcyclists can't be wrong . . .

in the 1984 model,' he says. 'The few things we didn't do for '84 will be included in the '85 model.' He remains a member of the design team, but project leadership for '85 has passed to another engineer, Hideaki Nebu. With five models to his credit, Mr Tanaka has held the post of GL project leader for longer than any other and in that time has presided over the most radical improvements in the machine's history. One improvement he still hopes to include is wireless headphones for the radio/cassette player, but the radio manufacturers are having problems with interference. Mr Tanaka had also hoped to develop a Honda trailer for the Gold Wing, but costs proved to be too high.

Sales of the 1200 are expected to top 25,000 units in the United States in 1984, 4500 in Canada and 3500 elsewhere, reflecting the predominance of the North American market in Honda's development of the Gold Wing.

Whether the 1200 stays with us for another five years before next undergoing redesign, or is altered radically before then, it is certain to continue as an institution in the motorcycle touring world. New competitors will come and go, but until such time as rival designers discover a better way of getting two people and their luggage across a continent on two wheels in style and comfort, the Gold Wing will remain the standard by which all touring motorcycles must be judged.

Index